WAR BRIDE

A full-length play by
Samantha Macher

Japanese Translations by
Sachiko Hayashi

CAST OF CHARACTERS

CATHERINE RHODES, The brilliant mother of a young soldier returning home from World War II
RICHARD LINDSTROM, A long-time friend to Catherine, the conductor of the local train station

THE PRICHETTS:

EVELYN PRICHETT, An idealistic young woman waiting for her soldier to come home. A maker of delicious pies.
NELLIE PRICHETT, Evelyn's sister. She too makes a delicious pie.
~and~
LUCILLE PRICHETT, Their mother and the town gossip.

~Also~

ALVIN RHODES, Catherine's son who has recently returned from the campaign in the Pacific with an eye-injury. In the first act, he wears a gauze bandage, in the second, an eye patch.
YUMI RHODES, His War Bride

In addition to the main cast there will be a group of dancers/actors hereafter known as: THE GHOSTS

TIME

Act I: October, 1945, Two months after the bombing of Hiroshima and Nagasaki
Act II: January, 1945, four months after the surrender of Japan to the Allies.

PLACE

Merced, California. A train stop, and then Catherine's home.

4

WAR BRIDE
© Samantha Macher
Trade Edition, 2015
ISBN 978-1-63092-075-3

Also Available By
Samantha Macher

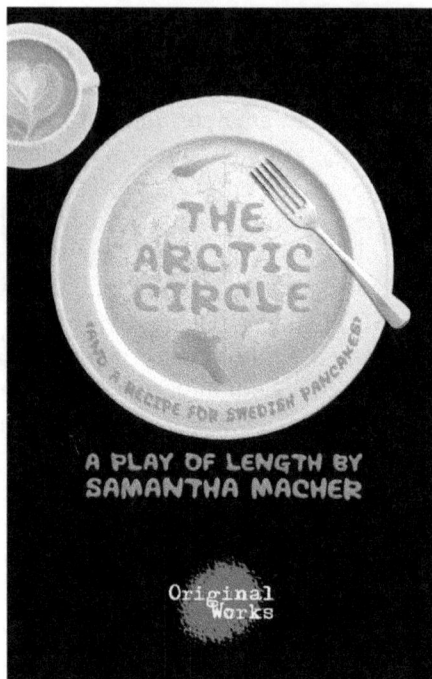

<u>THE ARCTIC CIRCLE</u>
<u>(and a recipe for Swedish pancakes)</u>

Synopsis: A Brechtian comedy about a woman in a troubled marriage who travels through time, space and Sweden to reexamine her past relationships for solutions to her newly found troubles. Unable to get the clear answers she needs, she must look inside herself to find what she is looking for.

Cast Size: 3 Males, 2 Females

The World Premiere of WAR BRIDE was produced in August of 2012 at SkyPilot Theatre in Los Angeles, California. It was directed and choreographed by Nancy Dobbs Owen. The Stage Manager was Heidi Marie, and her Assistant Stage Manager was Jude Evans. The set designers were Zachary B. Guiler and Cole Baldwin. The lighting was designed by Wes Chu. The sound designer was Matt Richter. The costume designer was Kareem Cervantes. The play was dramaturged by Rebecca Quirk and Sachiko Hayashi.

Original Cast:
Catherine Rhodes- Julia Sanford
Richard Lindstrom- Jeffrey Markle
Alvin Rhodes- Brett Fleisher
Yumi Rhodes- Sachiyo K
Evelyn Prichett- Amelia Rose
Nellie Prichett- Katie Apicella
Lucille Prichett- Kelly Goodman
Ghosts: Alicia Foo, Reesa Ishiyama, Yukari Koseki, and Ethan Zachery Scott

Understudies for extension:
Nellie Prichett Understudy- Allison Perkins
Ghost Understudy: Jude Evans

PLAYWRIGHT NOTES

All hyphenated Japanese should be read without taking a pause.

It is the playwright's intention that the Japanese text in the play is not meant to be fully understood by an American audience, if at all. Any projections with the English text (sub or supertitles, for example), would reveal too much about the ending of the play too soon.

In the original version of the play, this was handled by having the ghosts whisper the Japanese and the English text simultaneously under Yumi's lines, thus obfuscating the translation thereof. This practice resulted in the non-Japanese speaking audience members seeing, essentially, a different play than Japanese speakers. Any specific questions regarding the handling of this text should be directed to Original Works Publishing to be sent along to the playwright/ translator.

A NOTE ABOUT THE GHOSTS

They can be used in whatever form the director believes will add the most suspense and the most dread to the production without giving away the ending. They are best used in scenes that have both Yumi and Catherine in them.

SPECIAL THANKS

The playwright would like to thank Nancy Dobbs Owen and Heidi Marie for going above and beyond to make the show a success; SkyPilot Theatre Company and Jeff Goode for their dedication to this play, and for their mission of supporting new work in Los Angeles; The truly gifted actors for originating these roles; And finally, the designers/crew who made the play look like a million bucks (even though we spent less than $10K).

Additionally, she would like to thank Todd Ristau and the Playwright's Lab at Hollins University for helping to sponsor the production, Steven Stanley and Bill Raden for their continued support of her artistic efforts, Jason Aaron Goldberg and Dr. Steve Schachter for editing the play, and her parents for being incredible, supportive, people.

Finally, she would like to thank Sachiko Hayashi for her patience, friendship, and tireless work on this War Bride, both as an actor and a translator. ありがとう for everything.

WAR BRIDE

ACT I: SCENE ONE

A mother, Catherine Rhodes, stands on a train platform. She is waiting for her son, Alvin, to return from the war. She chats with a young woman, Evelyn.

CATHERINE: Now, he said in his letter that he'd be arriving on the three o'clock train.

EVELYN: Don't worry, I'm sure its coming.

CATHERINE: It's well past three now, Evelyn. I don't see any trains.

EVELYN: The train's always a little late, Mrs. Rhodes.

CATHERINE: Not this late.

EVELYN: There might've been cows on the track.

CATHERINE: And with a car of injured veterans. The way we run public transportation in this country is disgraceful.

EVELYN: Perhaps they were held up at the last station. Last minute passengers.

CATHERINE: Of course.

EVELYN: Or maybe they had to repair the engine. That takes some time. It would certainly cause the train to be late.

CATHERINE: I heard that in Europe that the trains run like clock-work.
　　　　Or rather, they did before all this unpleasantness.

EVELYN: Yes. That's probably it. Engine repair.

A long pause.

　　　　Or they got derailed and careened into a ditch.

CATHERINE: Excuse me?

EVELYN: Stranger things have happened, Mrs. Rhodes.

CATHERINE: Well that's true, but--

EVELYN: I heard about a train that went loose out in Jackson, Wyoming last summer where everyone aboard died on impact. Well, by that stop there were only about sixteen people on board, and they were mostly carrying coal, but still! All of them! DEAD!

CATHERINE: That is a terrible thing to have happened, but I'm quite sure that did not happen on this day to this train.

EVELYN: Well what if it did?

CATHERINE: Evelyn, I--

EVELYN: What if they are all dead? What if they're lying in the midst of the desert? Their fragile and injured bodies scattered across the sand--

CATHERINE: You need to stop this nonsense right now. I will not have it. My nerves are already ripped to ribbons!

EVELYN: Above them, the buzzards waiting, coveting the taste of human flesh in their hardened, yellow beaks. They hover, screeching away into the empty air with a CAW CAW!

CATHERINE: This is not at all lady-like, you know. To talk about carrion birds?

EVELYN: CAW! CAW CAW CAW! CAW!

CATHERINE: Evelyn.

EVELYN: CAW!

CATHERINE: Evelyn.

EVELYN: CAW CAW!

CATHERINE: Evelyn Prichett, that is ENOUGH.

The train arrives. Palpable relief.

See, the train is here. It's late, but it's here.

EVELYN: Thank my lucky stars. It's here!

CATHERINE: Yes, it is.

EVELYN: Oops! Oh no! All this chit chat and I forgot to powder my nose! Did I tell you Danny should be on this train?

CATHERINE: About a half-dozen times.

EVELYN: I'm going to run to the ladies to make sure I'm immaculate.

I'm so excited! Our boys! Our men. Heroes, Mrs. Rhodes, and they're home. I'm so very excited.

Even more so now that I know that the train didn't tragically derail, killing everyone aboard.

If you see Danny, will you grab him for me? Tell him that I'll be back in a jiff. Less than a jiff. Half a jiff. Three quarters of a jiff at most.

CATHERINE: If I see him, dear, I will.

Evelyn exits.

I'll be damned if she's not the strangest girl I ever met.

The train pulls into the station. A train station worker, Richard, walks up behind Catherine, and puts his hand on her shoulder. Catherine is scared to death (near-death, actually).

CATHERINE: OOF! Richard! Well I never! How dare you sneak up on me!

RICHARD: Who's sneaking? I simply saw a beautiful girl waiting on a platform for her soldier.

CATHERINE: You flatter me, Richard Lindstrom, you really do.

RICHARD: I hear your son's coming home today.

CATHERINE: Yes. He is.

RICHARD: You're a lucky woman.

CATHERINE: Apparently, he has some kind of injury.

RICHARD: Anything's better than coming home in a box, Catherine.

CATHERINE: I cannot even bear the thought of that.

RICHARD: He didn't tell you anything?

CATHERINE: Just that he was coming back. He didn't say much else in his letter.

RICHARD: A man of few words. Just like his--

CATHERINE: Don't remind me. I raised the boy practically on my own and he still manages to be Walter's double.

RICHARD: No matter how hard we fight it, boys do have a tendency to turn into their fathers.

CATHERINE: He says he has a surprise for me.

RICHARD: What do you think it is?

CATHERINE: I don't know. Could be anything, I suppose. I'm hoping for a tea set. The ones from the far east are quite lovely.

RICHARD: Do you think he'd have the time to shop for a tea set? He wasn't sightseeing in the Pacific, you know.

CATHERINE: You're a grouch, Richard.

RICHARD: I did fight in the Great War.

CATHERINE: How could I forget?

RICHARD: --and let me tell you, when you're down in the trenches, you don't have time to go shopping for tea sets for your mother.

She looks. She sees Alvin come off the train.

CATHERINE: Look! LOOK! There he is!

RICHARD: I can't see him--

CATHERINE: He's over there. *(To Richard)* He's home.

Richard grabs her hand.

ALVIN! ALVIN, over here, sweetheart!

She wildly waves her arm.

RICHARD: I see him! Alvin! OVER HERE!

CATHERINE: He doesn't hear us. ALVIN!

She releases the grip on Richard's hand.

Will you excuse me?

RICHARD: Of course.

She begins to exit.

CATHERINE: *(To Richard)* Goodbye, Richard.

RICHARD: Goodbye, Kitty! Oh! And good luck with that tea set.

CATHERINE: Don't call me Kitty.

Richard tips his cap to Catherine. She exits. Evelyn rushes on.

RICHARD: Well, hello again, Ms. Prichett, how are we doing--

EVELYN: Have the soldiers gotten off the train?

RICHARD: Yes.

EVELYN: I see. Are they all off yet?

RICHARD: Looks like the lot of them.

EVELYN: Oh.

RICHARD: Still waiting on your betrothed?

EVELYN: Yes, sir. Every day.

RICHARD: Every day at three o'clock.

EVELYN: We're to be married in June, and I have so many prepara-
tions to make--
    One day, he'll be here, won't he?

RICHARD: By the grace of God, I imagine. With a little help from
the US Army and the Zephyr train.

EVELYN: --Because I haven't heard from him. That is, I stopped
hearing from him. It's been so long since I--

RICHARD: I know, Evelyn. I know. A year and a half is a long time,
but not that unusual. The war just ended. You should take a few
days off. Wait for his letter--

EVELYN: But if what if he's injured? Or has amnesia? Or was in an
accident that blew off his hands and he can't write to me even
though he desperately yearns for just one pencil and a piece of--

RICHARD: Go home. Wait for his letter. Someday, hopefully soon,
he'll be back. Possibly on this very train.

EVELYN: You think so?

RICHARD: *(Beat.)* He'll come home.

EVELYN: Not today, though.

RICHARD: No. Not today. Today Alvin comes home.

EVELYN: That's good. For Mrs. Rhodes. She must be so happy.

RICHARD: She is.

EVELYN: *(Beat.)* Well. My mother's waiting for me. I should
probably go.

RICHARD: Tell her and your father I said hello.

EVELYN: I will, Mr. Lindstrom.

RICHARD: And thank your mother for that pie.

EVELYN: Yes, sir.

RICHARD: It's impossible to be a hungry widower in this town, although at the rate I'm being fed, I'll be too round to ever remarry.

He motions to his midsection.

EVELYN: In all the time we've known you, this is the first I've heard of remarriage--

RICHARD: It's gotten a bit lonely at the Lindstrom ranch these past few months. I feel ready to move on. I think Ruthie would have wanted that for me.

EVELYN: Well, then, I'll tell my mother to stop feeding you immediately. A nice fellow like you has no business being a bachelor this long.

RICHARD: Let's not be drastic. A man still needs his dessert.

EVELYN: Your future wife will thank me.

She pats his belly and then runs offstage. Richard shakes his head sadly.

RICHARD: I'm sure she will.

SCENE TWO

ALVIN, a young man in a military uniform and eye patch, unloads his bags from the side of a train. A young, Japanese woman, YUMI, stands beside him nervously. People pass by them. They look at her as one would look at a rotting corpse. She is surrounded by GHOSTS. Yumi says her lines in Japanese.

ALVIN: It's alright, Yumi, my mother is going to love you. You're going to be a part of the family.

YUMI: *Nikui.*
    (I hate you.)
    憎い。

ALVIN: Don't you love America already? It's so beautiful!
    The countryside, the mountains?
    Amber waves of grain?

YUMI: *Samishikute, karappono-tochi.*
    (Nothing but lonesome, empty fields.)
    寂しくて、空っぽの土地。

ALVIN: Now, I know it's a little intimidating, but soon, you'll fit right in, won't you my little darling?

She looks around her and everyone she sees looks strange to her. Men in uniforms. Women in Sunday dresses. Smoke from the train's engine.

YUMI: *Nihon-e kaeritai.*
    (I want to go home.)
    日本へ帰りたい。

ALVIN: Look. Here she comes.
    Put on that pretty smile.
    You do remember how to smile, don't you?
    Just use those little muscles in your cheeks--

He smiles at her, nodding, as if to say "you too." She does. He sticks his fingers in her dimples.

    And show me those teeth.

YUMI: *Watashito wakareru-tokiwa, nidoto warae-naiyo.*
(When I am done with you, you'll never smile again.)
私と別れる時は、二度と笑えないよ。

ALVIN: Looks good on you.

Yumi holds her smile the way someone would hold a live grenade.
Catherine enters.

CATHERINE: Alvin--
Oh my stars.

ALVIN: Mother!

Alvin wraps his confounded mother in a lengthy embrace.

It's good to see you.

CATHERINE: It is good to see you too.

She surrenders to the embrace, and then, pulling back--

What happened? Your eye! My baby!

ALVIN: I'm fine.

CATHERINE: What happened?

ALVIN: I really don't want to talk about it now.

CATHERINE: But--

ALVIN: I have someone I want you to meet.

CATHERINE: Alright.

Alvin motions for Yumi to come meet Catherine. Her stomach
drops. For the rest of the play, Catherine is never unaware of Yumi.

ALVIN: Mother, this is Yumi.

CATHERINE: Yumi?

ALVIN: My wife.

Catherine laughs.

What?

CATHERINE: Your wife. What are you talking about, Alvin?

ALVIN: We're married.

CATHERINE: You can't be. How are you married?

ALVIN: We married overseas. Many of us took a bride--

Catherine goes white as a sheet.

CATHERINE: Alvin. I-- I don't understand. Is this some kind of sick joke?

ALVIN: Excuse me?

CATHERINE: Tell me. Tell me that you're lying to me. Tell me that this Jap is not your wife.

ALVIN: We met on Okinawa--

CATHERINE: Okinawa?

ALVIN: She was a great help to me after the accident--

CATHERINE: A great help to you? Help?

ALVIN: --and it was love at first sight.

CATHERINE: Love at first sight?

ALVIN: *(Motioning to his eye)* Well, maybe not sight.

He laughs.

CATHERINE: Oh, Alvin. Oh my gracious, Alvin. What have you done?

ALVIN: Mother--

CATHERINE: This is treason, do you know that? Treason, Alvin!

ALVIN: Please. You're being hysterical.

CATHERINE: Hysterical--

ALVIN: *(Ignoring Catherine)* Yumi, this is my mother. We're going to be staying with her for a little while until we get our own home someday. *(To Catherine)* If that's okay? It's okay with you, isn't it, mother?

CATHERINE: Of course it is not okay!

ALVIN: Mother, please? We just got here. We have nowhere to go.

CATHERINE: Well that's a shame. You should have thought of that before you went and married her! You should have thought about so many things!

ALVIN: Well, I didn't think you'd turn me out.

CATHERINE: Turn you out? I'm not turning you out. I'm turning her out.

ALVIN: The war is over, mother. We won--

CATHERINE: Over? Hardly!

ALVIN: The bomb--

CATHERINE: And you don't think they want revenge?

ALVIN: You're joking.

CATHERINE: And even so, why would a woman like her marry an American soldier?

ALVIN: Mother--

CATHERINE: And at her age.

ALVIN: You're making a scene--

CATHERINE: Me? I'm making a scene? You bring home a little China Doll for the whole town to see and then accuse me of making a scene?

ALVIN: Stop it!

CATHERINE: No! I'm sorry. There's some things I can't stand for. And this. This? This is one of them. I'm leaving.

Catherine tries to exit.

ALVIN: Mother?

Alvin blocks her.

CATHERINE: No. Let me go.

ALVIN: Mother, we have nowhere to go.

He grips her tightly.

CATHERINE: Alvin, let go! You're hurting me.

ALVIN: It won't be for very long. I promise.

CATHERINE: Ouch, Alvin! Let go of me!

ALVIN: I promise.

Alvin stares at his mother. He grips her, tightly. Total silence.

And you don't have to worry about Yumi. Not one bit. She's gentler than a springtime lamb.

Alvin releases Catherine and caresses Yumi.

Please.
I'm your son.

CATHERINE: *(Beat.)* Fine.

ALVIN: Fine, what?

CATHERINE: FINE. You can come home with me.

ALVIN: Thank you so very much. You won't even notice us--

CATHERINE: Enough. Does she even speak English?

ALVIN: Not yet, but she'll learn.

CATHERINE: But you speak with her in--

ALVIN: It's an immersion technique I learned in the Army. She'll catch on soon, I swear it.

CATHERINE: She doesn't even speak the language? Not at all? Not even a little?

ALVIN: I said she'll learn.

CATHERINE: I'm not comfortable with this. I'm not comfortable with this at all.

ALVIN: It will be fine.

CATHERINE: What if she's--

ALVIN: Whatever you think she is, she's not. I promise.

Alvin takes Catherine's hands. Catherine nods in agreement.

I'm going to get our things from the platform. Why don't you two get to know one another?

CATHERINE: Fine.

ALVIN: I'll be right back.

Alvin exits.

CATHERINE: Yumi, welcome.

She extends her hand. An explosion of cherry blossoms. Yumi is menacing. The Ghosts are terrifying.

CATHERINE: *(Fearfully)* It's so nice to meet you.

The kitchen of the Rhodes household. Catherine is clearing the table. Yumi looks on, sitting uncomfortably, while Alvin relaxes in his chair.

ALVIN: ...So, when I wake up, I see Yumi, in her nurse's uniform, looking like a vision, you should have seen it, I swear, she stood like an angel above me, and as I came out of the fog, I knew, I just knew I had to have her.
　　　　I had to make her my wife--

CATHERINE: What a lovely story.

ALVIN: And you should have seen the way she looked at me, Mother, it was like I was some kind of American movie star. I knew I had to have looked hideous, but she went crazy for me, almost like a lovesick teenager.

Catherine notices Yumi's expression. So does Alvin. He is not happy with her demeanor.

CATHERINE: I am glad to see you still send her after all these--
　　　　How long did you say it had been? Since you met her? How long was it?

ALVIN: Two months--

CATHERINE: Ah. Well then. After all these months.

ALVIN: I have something for you. A gift?

CATHERINE: Another surprise. How wonderful. What now? Is your yellow wife in a family way?

ALVIN: Not yet. And I would thank you not to be sarcastic with me. This is a special occasion.

CATHERINE: It certainly is.

ALVIN: I don't have to give it to you. The present I brought you. Would you like it or not?

CATHERINE: It depends.

ALVIN: On what, exactly?

CATHERINE: On whether or not it's a tea set.

ALVIN: It's better than a tea set.

Alvin leaves the room. Yumi glares at Catherine. They make bone-chilling eye-contact.

YUMI: *Hidoi-tabemono. Konoie-hakikega-suru.*
(This food is terrible. Your home is disgusting.)
ひどい食べ物。この家吐き気がする。

CATHERINE: What?

Alvin reenters with a box. Catherine keeps her eyes glued firmly to Yumi.

ALVIN: For you, Mother.

He hands it to her. She holds it but does not open it.

CATHERINE: Thank you.

ALVIN: Aren't you going to open it?

CATHERINE: Of course. Of course I will.

She does. She unwraps the gift from a bed of tissue paper. She holds up a belt, a thousand-stitch belt. Alvin looks at Yumi.

YUMI: *Chikushoo.*
(You terrible bastard.)
畜生。

ALVIN: So. What do you think?

CATHERINE: I'm not sure. What is it?

ALVIN: It's a thousand-stitch belt. Wives of soldiers in the Japanese army make them for their husbands. They wear them under their uniforms. Right up against the skin. They believe it makes them invincible.

YUMI: *Kono chikusho-yaroo.*
    (You terrible bastard.)
    この畜生野郎。

CATHERINE: What did she say?

ALVIN: She says she wanted you to have it.

CATHERINE: But, why?

ALVIN: She made it for me after we fell in love.

CATHERINE: Then why should I have it? It is yours, right? You should have it.

She tries to hand it back to Alvin. He will not let her.

ALVIN: She thinks it will help remind you of just how much she loves me.

He looks at Yumi.

CATHERINE: She doesn't seem happy about this.

ALVIN: It was her idea. Why shouldn't she be happy?

CATHERINE: I don't know, but look at her face--

ALVIN: She's just nervous.

CATHERINE: Alvin, I--

ALVIN: Please, Mother. Take the gift. It's irreplaceable.

She holds it up. She notices a blood stain.

CATHERINE: What is--

ALVIN: Oh, that. It's from my injuries, I'll have Yumi wash it.

CATHERINE: My stars--

ALVIN: If she washes it, will you take it? Please?

CATHERINE: Yes. Of course. Thank you.

ALVIN: You're welcome.

CATHERINE: Thank you, Yumi.

Yumi looks away.

>She's something of a shrinking violet, isn't she?
>Are you ready for dessert? I made cherry Jello.

ALVIN: My favorite.

CATHERINE: Wonderful.

Catherine plops a bowl full of cherry Jello down in front of Yumi.

>For you.

YUMI: *Iranai.*
>(I do not want your food.)
>いらない。

CATHERINE: What did she say?

YUMI: *Iranaitte-itteruno.*
>(I do not want your food.)
>いらないって言ってるの。

ALVIN: She appears to have lost her appetite

CATHERINE: But there's always room for Jello.

ALVIN: She says she's full.

CATHERINE: So she won't be having any? None at all?

ALVIN: I suppose not.

CATHERINE: Well, she should at least try it. It's impolite.

ALVIN: You're right. She should try it.

CATHERINE: I think she would like it.

YUMI: *Omaetachino-tabemonowa-tabetakunai. Kokode-netakunai.*
(I do not want to eat your food. To sleep in your home.)
お前たちの食べ物は食べたくない。ここで寝たくない。

CATHERINE: What now?

ALVIN: She says that she's very tired.

CATHERINE: Well she doesn't need my permission to leave the table. If she doesn't want dessert, that's fine by me.

ALVIN: She should at least have a bite.

CATHERINE: Well, don't force the girl--

ALVIN: Come on, darling. Take a bite. Just one. Please.

He puts a spoonful of Jello in front of her face.

It's delicious.

YUMI: *Yamete.*
(No.)
やめて。

She stands up and leaves the table.

CATHERINE: I guess she doesn't like sweets.

Alvin follows her.

SCENE FOUR

Catherine sits at the table. It is evening. She is stirring a cup of coffee. There is a newspaper spread in front of her. A knock at the kitchen door. It startles her. She composes herself quickly.

CATHERINE: I'm coming!

She answers. Richard is at the door.

RICHARD: Good evening, Mrs. Rhodes.

CATHERINE: Richard, that is twice in one day that you have startled me.

RICHARD: Is this a bad time? I came by to welcome home the conquering hero.

CATHERINE: No.
       It's just.
       He's asleep.
       They're asleep.

RICHARD: They are?

CATHERINE: What? Don't tell me you haven't heard yet? Alvin is married now. To a little yellow tramp.

RICHARD: Perhaps, I should just come back tomorrow.

Richard tries to leave.

CATHERINE: No. Don't. It's just--
       I apologize.
       Would you like to come in?

RICHARD: Are you sure?

Catherine nods and pulls open the door wide. Richard enters.

CATHERINE: Please, sit down. Wherever you want.

He does.

CATHERINE (Cont'd): Coffee?

RICHARD: I would like that.

She begins to fix him a cup of coffee.

CATHERINE: I don't have any cream. And I only have a little bit of my sugar ration left, but I might have some nutmeg, and that's almost as good if you ask me--

RICHARD: Actually, I'll just take it black.

Catherine looks at Richard skeptically.

> I like it black.
> Honestly.

CATHERINE: But you even sugar everything. I've seen you sugar pie.

RICHARD: What can I say? I like my pie sweet and my coffee black.

CATHERINE: --

RICHARD: Speaking of which, do you have any pie? I haven't eaten in hours.

Catherine sighs and pulls out a dish of Jello.

CATHERINE: This is the best I can do.

She plops it down in front of Richard.

RICHARD: It looks. Delicious.

CATHERINE: I made it for Alvin. It's his favorite.

RICHARD: I bet he thoroughly enjoyed it.

CATHERINE: He likes cherry.

RICHARD: Nothing better than cherry Jello.

CATHERINE: I was saving it until he got home. The girl hardly even looked at it. It was the strangest thing--

RICHARD: Oh?

CATHERINE: I thought everyone liked Jello.

RICHARD: You did?

CATHERINE: You know what I mean.

RICHARD: Of course.

CATHERINE: And the worst thing of all was that I was actually trying a little bit. To be kind--
I still cannot believe him.

RICHARD: Alvin?
Yes, Alvin.

RICHARD: His judgment does seem to be a bit questionable on this one, doesn't it?

CATHERINE: I don't know what in heaven's name he was thinking.

RICHARD: I'm not sure.

CATHERINE: Of all the women he could have chosen--

RICHARD: He chose her.

CATHERINE: She's the enemy for goodness sake.

RICHARD: She was anyway.

CATHERINE: Fine. Until practically a minute ago she was the enemy, and now suddenly, I'm to believe she's not? She doesn't even speak the language.

RICHARD: And yet, she's the talk of the town.

CATHERINE: It isn't funny, Richard.

RICHARD: I never said it was.

CATHERINE: Don't be cute.

RICHARD: I apologize if I offended you. I do.

A long pause. Richard stirs his coffee.

CATHERINE: Are we really the talk of the town?

RICHARD: Well, it's certainly more Alvin than you. Although you have lots of people wondering what you're doing with that girl in your house. After everything that's happened.

CATHERINE: Oh goodness.

RICHARD: You know, they sent me here to try talk some sense into Alvin.

CATHERINE: And who are they?

RICHARD: The concerned citizens of our fair city, of course.

CATHERINE: The Prichetts?

RICHARD: Well, of course. You know it wouldn't be proper if Lucille wasn't leading the brigade.

CATHERINE: This is a nightmare.

RICHARD: It's a worrisome thing for everyone, Catherine, you must try to be a little sympathetic towards--

CATHERINE: It's beyond worrisome. This is insanity.

RICHARD: They think she's a spy or something ridiculous like that.

CATHERINE: Well you can tell them all to join the club.

RICHARD: I mean it, Kitty, they sent these people to Manzanar in droves. Most of the town wouldn't even spit on a Jap if they were on fire.

CATHERINE: Count me in.

RICHARD: That's not good enough. To tell them all that. It's not a good enough answer.

CATHERINE: What do you want me to say?

RICHARD: I want to know what you want me to tell them. About the girl?

CATHERINE: Tell them all I don't know anything about it. That my house has been taken over. That I'm a hostage to my immature son, and a woman who is probably plotting her revenge as we speak.

RICHARD: I can't tell them that.

CATHERINE: I heard that that bomb--
That it was devastating Richard. I heard it was absolutely devastating. Who wouldn't want to take vengeance on the country that did that?

RICHARD: If I tell them what you just said, they'll be here with pitchforks and torches. Lucille leading the charge.

CATHERINE: Let them come. If they take her away, I might have a moment's peace.

RICHARD: They'll be coming for your son, too.

A long pause.

Look. I'll tell them whatever you want, you know that I will. I can even tell them all that I met her. That I'm suspicious, as are we all, but in time, maybe she'll prove to be, I don't know, a patriot. I'll tell them that she seems like a sweetheart.

CATHERINE: Oh yes, she's a real Tokyo Rose.

RICHARD: No. She's not.
Tokyo Rose speaks English.

Catherine begins to cry.

CATHERINE: Oh Richard, I--

RICHARD: What? What is it? What's wrong, Kitty?

CATHERINE: I'm--
> She scares me.

RICHARD: Why? Has she done something? Said something?

CATHERINE: No. Nothing like that. It's just.
> It's just--
> When I met her, when I stood across from her on that train platform, I felt ice cutting right through all of my bones. It cut them right to the marrow.

RICHARD: Oh boy. Aw geeze, Catherine. That's terrible, but I'm sure it's nothing. She probably doesn't know what to think, what to make of any of this.

CATHERINE: And on top of all that, just to add insult to injury, at dinner tonight, she looked at me with utter disdain when I put food in front of her.

RICHARD: Well--

CATHERINE: She didn't like my Jello, Richard.

Richard holds back laughter.

> What?

RICHARD: Nothing, it's just--

CATHERINE: What?

RICHARD: Nobody likes your Jello, Kitty. Not even me. Probably not even Alvin. For all your talents, milady, you're no Betty Crocker.
> You can't hold the Jello against her.

CATHERINE: Well I do.
> Sometimes, and I hate to admit it, Richard, I really do, but sometimes, I really wish Walter was here.

RICHARD: Oh?

31

CATHERINE: Yeah. He was a lousy husband, but I don't think he ever would have stood for all this nonsense with Alvin.

RICHARD: Why do you? Stand for it, I mean? If you need rules, Kitty, you need to lay them down now. Walt's not coming back.

A gaping pause. Catherine looks away.

CATHERINE: You really don't like my Jello?

RICHARD: Well. Would you look at the time?

CATHERINE: Richard!

RICHARD: It is rather late, and I am not long for bed.

He stands up from the table.

CATHERINE: Answer me, this minute.

RICHARD: I love your Jello because you made it.
	Or mixed it.
	Or did whatever it was that you do to get it to turn from a powder into a bright-red bowl of gel.

CATHERINE: Thank you.

RICHARD: Anytime.

CATHERINE: And thank you for coming by.

RICHARD: It's my pleasure.

He stands up.

CATHERINE: And tell everyone--
	Tell them all--

RICHARD: I'll tell them that you have it under control. That everything is fine. I will. I'll tell them.

CATHERINE: Thank you.

He turns to leave, but remembers--

RICHARD: You know, Sheriff Regan at the station may have a Japanese dictionary from when he worked down south.

CATHERINE: So?

RICHARD: I can see if he'll lend it to you.

CATHERINE: For what?

RICHARD: To try and talk to her.

CATHERINE: Now why would I want to do such a thing?

RICHARD: Because if you can understand her, even a little, it might make you feel better. If nothing else, it'll let her know that you're paying attention to her, and if she's good, you'll learn nothing but wonderful, reassuring truths. And if she's bad, well--

He makes a throat-cutting motion.

> I'll bring it by this week.
> Come on, Kitty, try it.
> You'll feel better.

Richard opens the door to go. Catherine stands up.

CATHERINE: You should get on home. Lucille Prichett's probably timing your visit as we speak.

RICHARD: Undoubtedly.
> Goodnight, Kitty.

He leaves.

CATHERINE: Goodnight, Richard. *(Calling after him)* And stop calling me Kitty!

She sits back down and nervously looks around. She reads the paper. She looks around again. She sees Yumi. The lights change. Catherine looks down at her newspaper and finds that it has all turned to small, paper cranes.

33

Morning at the Rhodes household. Catherine has fallen asleep at the table. The cranes have vanished. The newspaper is restored. Alvin enters and gently tries to wakes her.

ALVIN: Mother?

He shakes her a bit on the shoulder.

Mother, wake up. It's morning.

Catherine wakes up.

CATHERINE: Oh! Alvin?
Alvin!
What time is it?

ALVIN: It's just before six.

CATHERINE: What are you doing up?

ALVIN: I heard from Tom at the lumberyard yesterday and he told me to stop in and see about getting back to work.

CATHERINE: Wonderful.

ALVIN: Since you would like me out of the house as soon as possible, I thought it would be good of me to take him up on his offer.

CATHERINE: You're right. That would be good.

ALVIN: There's a management position open.

CATHERINE: Are you sure you're even eligible? Your family circumstances have changed a bit--

ALVIN: Right now they have a bunch of women holding down the fort. I'm sure they'll be glad to have a rooster in that hen house.

CATHERINE: Of course.
Can I make you something to eat before you leave me here alone with that woman for hours?

ALVIN: Mother, enough. It's too early for this--

CATHERINE: You can't well go to that job interview on an empty stomach. I want you at your best. Can't I fix you some eggs?

ALVIN: Just coffee, thanks.

CATHERINE: It would only take me a--

ALVIN: No. Thank you.

She fixes the coffee. Alvin looks at the newspaper.

CATHERINE: Richard Lindstrom was by last night to see you.

ALVIN: And how is old Dick?

CATHERINE: He is fine. He wanted to greet the conquering hero and meet his little woman.

ALVIN: And why might he want to do such a thing?

CATHERINE: Oh, you know Richard. He checks in on everybody.

ALVIN: Of course.

CATHERINE: Are you free some night this week? He'd love to stop by.

ALVIN: Tell him any time after six this week is good, when you see him.

CATHERINE: I will.

She puts the coffee down on the table.

Alvin?

ALVIN: Yes?

CATHERINE: I want you to know--

ALVIN: What?

CATHERINE: I'm glad to have you home.

ALVIN: You have a funny way of showing it.

CATHERINE: I'm not apologizing for my reservations, Alvin. I'm not. That woman is trouble. I feel it--

ALVIN: I won't have you speak of my wife that way.

CATHERINE: Fine. I won't. I'll just speak of her people, who we have hauled away from here by the hundreds trying to keep our country safe.

ALVIN: Good God--

CATHERINE: You will not take the Lord's name in vain here.

ALVIN: I will do as I please.

CATHERINE: Some things, like God, like country, are sacred. Not that you care.

ALVIN: Care? Care? I gave my eye for this place. Don't you tell me anything about caring--

CATHERINE: I am sorry. You're right. That was insensitive.

ALVIN: I'm blind.

CATHERINE: And I said that I am sorry!

A pause.

Does Tom know?

ALVIN: Does Tom know what?

CATHERINE: About your injury?

ALVIN: It's not important.

CATHERINE: Well--

ALVIN: It's a management position. Not labor. You don't need both eyes if you're not labor.

CATHERINE: Then the interview should be a piece of cake.

ALVIN: Yes, it should.

CATHERINE: Good.

ALVIN: That is what you want, isn't it? Unless of course you'd rather I stay home with you and Yumi.

CATHERINE: That would be preferable to leaving me with her all day. Yes.

ALVIN: I see. So you want me to stay home with you. Hm? Like a little boy with a new house pet? Like a woman with a child? Why is that? Because you're scared of her?

CATHERINE: Yes. I am.

ALVIN: Because her slanty eyes make you nervous?

CATHERINE: Alvin, that is not appropriate.

ALVIN: Because her yellow skin doesn't match the doilies?

CATHERINE: There's no need to take that tone with me, Alvin--

ALVIN: Tone? What tone? This has been the tone of the whole conversation.

CATHERINE: I was merely saying that--

ALVIN: After I spent the last three years fighting for my country, you want me to stay home and babysit?

CATHERINE: Yes.
Maybe for a few days. I can return to work--

ALVIN: You don't need to work anymore. There's finally a man in this house.

CATHERINE: I have been supporting this household for longer than you've been out of diapers--

ALVIN: You're a silly woman.

CATHERINE: I beg your pardon!

ALVIN: Can't you just accept that I would like to take care of you?

CATHERINE: Well, then how do you suggest I care for my home once you and your wife find other accommodations? Hmm?
     I am sorry, Alvin. If it had just been you, you could stay forever if you wanted, but I didn't know that this was what you were expecting of me. You gave me no warning, no indication that you were bringing home a--

ALVIN: A what? Wife? Well, I'm sorry. I really am.
    Sorry that you are a bigot.

CATHERINE: You will not speak to me like that in my home.

ALVIN: Well that's just swell. In fact, it works out perfectly because I'm leaving.

CATHERINE: Now wait just one hot second--

ALVIN: I'm late.

CATHERINE: We are not done with this conversation!

Yumi appears.

YUMI: *Naze kenka-shiteru? Konohito-shitteruno? Nanio?*
    (Why are they fighting? Does she know? What does she know?)
    なぜ喧嘩してる？　この人知ってるの？　何を？

ALVIN: *(Noticing Yumi)* See what you've done? You woke her up.

CATHERINE: Alvin, I--

He leaves. Slamming the door. Both Yumi and Catherine shudder.

SCENE SIX

A knock at the kitchen door.

CATHERINE : I'm coming.

Another knock.

I'm coming.

Another knock.

Hold your horses, already. Goodness gracious.

Catherine enters. She is in her midday shopping outfit. She opens the door and sees Evelyn, Evelyn's sister, Nellie, and their mother, Lucille.

EVELYN: Welcome Wagon!

Catherine slams the door and leans against it.
A gentle knock.

LUCILLE (OFF): Catherine? Catherine! We know you're in there.

EVELYN (OFF): Open up, you silly goose!

NELLIE (OFF): We brought you pie.

CATHERINE: *(To herself)* My goodness. You'd think the women in this town have nothing better to do than bake pie.
   (To the women) One second, ladies, I'm fixing my hair.

She takes a deep breath and opens the door.

Oh the Prichetts. What a wonderful surprise.

EVELYN: We're not a surprise, Mrs. Rhodes, you just saw us a second ago!

CATHERINE: Well--

LUCILLE: Evelyn told us the, uh, wonderful news!

39

NELLIE: That Alvin is home.

LUCILLE: Richard told us that he has gotten married--

NELLIE: To a foreigner--

EVELYN: And we got ever so excited--

NELLIE: Well, Evelyn did. I was mostly just suspicious--

LUCILLE: You know we always thought your Alvin would marry my Nellie, especially after she was his homecoming queen, but things do change, I suppose.

EVELYN: But Mr. Lindstrom told us that he got to meet her yesterday, and she seemed upstanding.

LUCILLE: He said that she has Ally sympathies.

NELLIE: I think she's a spy, personally. I don't care what Richard Lindstrom says. He's nothing but a--

EVELYN: Nellie, quit it! You're being impolite.

LUCILLE: She's right, dear, it's impolite. Even if we all think that she is absolutely a dirty, filthy, Japanese spy, you can't just say it aloud.

NELLIE: But I didn't get to finish! You never let me think my thoughts.

EVELYN: Alright. Finish.

NELLIE: Well, I don't remember now.

EVELYN: Well--

CATHERINE: Well--

LUCILLE: Well, we decided to bake a pie.

NELLIE: Each of us baked a pie, actually.

LUCILLE: So that we could come by and meet the new Mrs. Rhodes—

EVELYN: Mrs. Alvin Rhodes.

CATHERINE: You shouldn't have.

LUCILLE: Don't be silly. Of course we should have.

EVELYN: I made apple. Because her new husband is an American hero. And nothing's more American than apple pie, right?

LUCILLE: And Nellie baked--

NELLIE: --A cherry pie. Like a cherry blossom? It might make Alvin's new wife feel like she's right back in Japan.

EVELYN: And Mother baked--

LUCILLE: --A pudding pie. A chocolate pudding pie.
      From a boxed mix.
      I would have made something better but the girls were hogging my stove.
      And they used up all my sugar rations.

CATHERINE: You didn't have to do that. Any of that. I still have leftover Jello from dinner last night.

EVELYN: Well we just thought it might make the girl feel more welcome.

LUCILLE: And with as often as Mr. Lindstrom has been coming by--

CATHERINE: Did he tell you that?

NELLIE: And we know how he loves his pies.

CATHERINE: Yes, I'm--

EVELYN: And we also know you don't cook much, so we thought these would be nice just to have around the house.

CATHERINE: I cook. Did Richard tell you I don't cook? Because I cook. All the time.

41

The Prichetts laugh.

LUCILLE: Oh, Catherine, coffee? Jello?

CATHERINE: He told you that?

LUCILLE: When I went by to bring him his lunch, he told me how grateful he was just to have a home-cooked meal--

CATHERINE: Oh did he, now?

LUCILLE: He told me he'd been by to visit this week and left with a grumbling tummy.

CATHERINE: I'll give him something else to grumble about the next time I see him.

EVELYN: Oh! And don't forget Mother--

NELLIE: Yes, don't forget, he gave us something to bring Mrs. Rhodes.

CATHERINE: He did? What is it?

LUCILLE: Well I don't know. I certainly don't go poking through people's parcels. I'm not a snoop, you know--

CATHERINE: Of course.

LUCILLE: Evelyn, give Mrs. Rhodes her package.

Evelyn goes through her purse and pulls out two small books wrapped in brown paper.

CATHERINE: I wonder what it could be.

They all stare at Catherine, hoping she'll open the package.

I'll just have to open it later. I'm on my way to the market.

EVELYN: Is Alvin's new wife coming with you?

NELLIE: Yes, is she?

CATHERINE: Well--

EVELYN: We're dying to meet her--

NELLIE: We hear she's beautiful, even if she's selling our secrets to a foreign government--

LUCILLE: Girls, girls! Let's not keep Mrs. Rhodes from her chores.

EVELYN: Of course.

NELLIE: We apologize.

CATHERINE: I'll tell you what.

EVELYN: Yes?

CATHERINE: I need a few hours next week to myself to run a few errands. I know Yumi might be a bit lonely and--

NELLIE: Her name is Yumi?

EVELYN: How Oriental!

CATHERINE: And if you wouldn't mind lending me your girls, Lucy--

LUCILLE: Lucille--

CATHERINE: Lucille, I'd love to have them come by and teach Yumi how to make one of her famous pies for Alvin. It will help her to, um, adjust, to being here in California.

NELLIE: Anything we can do.

EVELYN: It's like being a part of the war effort! Danny's going to be so proud.

CATHERINE: Exactly.

LUCILLE: We need to make friends with her so she won't call in a bomb strike here in our city.

CATHERINE: You know what they say "Good pies make good friends."

NELLIE: Do they?

EVELYN: Yes, Nellie. I have it embroidered on a pillow in my room.

CATHERINE: That's, well, that's--
　　　　Isn't that just something.

EVELYN: We'll be friends in no time.

LUCILLE: Well, we don't want to hold you up from the market.

EVELYN: And I actually need to get down to the train stop.

CATHERINE: Are you meeting Danny today?

EVELYN: I think so. Today should be the day.

NELLIE: She says that every day.

CATHERINE: And someday, it will be.
　　　　Maybe even today.

They all fall quiet.

　　　　Someday, he will, Evvie.

EVELYN: I know.

NELLIE: We should go.

LUCILLE: Alright, ladies! And we're off!

CATHERINE: Good day, Lucille.

LUCILLE: Goodbye!

NELLIE: Goodbye!

EVELYN: Enjoy the desserts.

CATHERINE: I will. Thank you.

The Prichetts (and their infectious hospitality) exit. Catherine rests. She looks at the parcel and opens it.

Dictionaries? Ugh, Richard.

She puts them on the table disgusted. She stares at it. She rolls her eyes, trying to ignore it. She thinks about it for a second.

He seriously thinks I'm going to talk to this girl--

She picks one of them up and thumbs through it.

Just look at all this, it's completely ridiculous--

She stops on a page.

Konnichiwa.
Pfft.

She sounds it out.

Ko-nee-chee-wah.

She perfects it.

Konnichiwa.

She calls Yumi, nervously.

Yumi? Yumi! Can you come here a minute?
Why would you ask that, it's not like she understands you.

Yumi appears. Surrounded by ghosts.

Yumi? Uh--
(Reading) Ko-nee-chee-wah?
My ridiculous and apparently insane friend Richard told me that I should try to talk to you. So that you think I can understand you. So that I can spy on you, because I'll be damned if you think you're going to spy on me--

He brought me these. Shall we give it the old college try?

45

She shows her the dictionary.

YUMI : *Aa nikui. Nikushimide, konochiga-nietagitteru. Urameshii. Anta, kono-tochi, antano-musukoga... Kaminosaki-kara tsumasaki-made, furuega-tomaranai.*
> (I despise you. I despise you with all the blood in my body. I despise you all the way down to the tiniest part of myself. I loathe you. This place. Your son. All they way down to my fingernails, and the tips of my hair.)
> ああ憎い。憎しみで、この血が煮えたぎってる。怨めしい。アンタ、この土地、アンタの息子が・・・髪の先からつま先まで震えが止まらない。

CATHERINE: I'll take that as a no.

Catherine goes back to her dictionary.

> This is silly. Konnichiwa? Perhaps, um--
> *(Reading)* Ohayou?
> Is that right?

YUMI: *Konnichiwa.*

CATHERINE:　Oh! Konnichiwa! Wonderful. See, we're talking? Konnichiwa, Hello!

Yumi takes the book and looks through it.

YUMI: He-lo-ou.

Catherine is dumbfounded.

CATHERINE: Yes, Yumi! Hello. Hello!

YUMI: *Nani? Watashito-hanashitai? Iiwa, demo ozomashii-koto-bakariyo.　Soredemo-iino?*
> (Is this what you want? To talk to me? Fine. But what I have to say is unpleasant. You will not like it.)
> 何？　私と話したい？　いいわ、でもおぞましい事ばかりよ。それでもいいの？

She hands her a paper crane.

CATHERINE: Oh my! Oh my goodness. How? How lovely. Thank you.

Catherine thumbs through the dictionary and looks up "Thank You."

>   Doumo. Thank you.

YUMI: *Nihongoga kantanto-omounara, soreo-akete, nakao-yondemite.*
>   (If you think you know so much Japanese, open the crane.
>   Read what's inside.)
>   日本語が簡単と思うなら、それを開けて中 を読んでみ
>   て。

CATHERINE: Thank you so much.

An explosion of cherry blossoms backed by the sound of brutal gun-fire.

SCENE SEVEN

Lights up on a domestic scene. Yumi in the kitchen with the Prichett girls. Catherine washes dishes behind them.

EVELYN: So the first thing you need to do once you make the dough, is put flour on the table so that when you roll it out, it doesn't stick.

Evelyn puts flour on the table. She motions to Yumi to do the same. She does.

NELLIE: Then, you want to roll out the dough slowly and carefully. You don't want to break it.

Nellie mimes rolling the dough, and then hands the rolling pin to Yumi. Yumi tries.

> Slower than that! And more gently--
> Gently!
> GENT--
> Argh!

Yumi does not understand. She looks at Nellie, confused.

> Mrs. Rhodes, do you know the Japanese word for gentle?

CATHERINE: No.

EVELYN: She doesn't speak Japanese, goodness gracious.

NELLIE: It can't hurt to ask.

CATHERINE: Why don't you use the dictionary that Mr. Lindstrom brought me? It's on the counter.

EVELYN: So it was a book. I told you, Nellie. I told you it was a book. Nellie thought it was a stack of love letters.

Evelyn goes and gets the book.

CATHERINE: Mr. Lindstrom likely isn't capable of writing a grocery list, let alone a stack of love letters.

NELLIE: Well, that isn't what I thought, anyway, Evvie.

EVELYN: Yes it was.

NELLIE: No it wasn't.

EVELYN: I heard you, Nellie! With my own two ears. I heard you say that you thought it was a book of love letters. Romantic ones. Ones with kissing, Mrs. Rhodes, you should have heard her--

CATHERINE: *(Aside)* Yes, that'll certainly be the day--

Catherine goes back to washing dishes.

NELLIE: Evelyn Marie Prichett, I said no such thing--

EVELYN: You did so.

NELLIE: I did not.

EVELYN: You're lying!

NELLIE: No I'm not. YOU'RE lying.

She slams the rolling pin down accidentally on Yumi's hands. Yumi screams.

Oh no. Oh my goodness!

EVELYN: Now, see what you've gone and done! *(To Yumi)* Yumi? Are you okay?

NELLIE: Oh my goodness, I'm so sorry--

CATHERINE: What on earth did you do?

EVELYN: Nellie slammed that rolling pin down on Yumi's hand. You're so clumsy, Nellie--

NELLIE: Where's the dictionary? I need to look up how to say I'm sorry!

CATHERINE: Oh my goodness. Yumi--

She takes out the dictionary.

> *Itai desu ka?* (You hurt?)

YUMI: *Itai! Yubiga!*
(Ouch! My fingers!)
痛い、指が！

Her fingers are broken.

CATHERINE: She needs a doctor.

Nellie steals the dictionary from Catherine, and looks through it.

NELLIE: *AYAMARE!!* (APOLOGIZE!!)

YUMI: *Ayamare?*
(Apologize?)
あやまれ？

She becomes frightened.

CATHERINE: What did you just say?

NELLIE: I think I said "sorry--"
AYAMARE! (APOLOGIZE!)

YUMI: *Gomennasai?*
(I'm sorry?)
ごめんなさい？

She grips her hands and wails.

CATHERINE: I'm going to call the doctor. Evelyn, get her some ice, wrap it up in a towel--

Catherine leaves. Evelyn gets up to get ice. Yumi grabs her dress pleadingly.

EVELYN: I think you'd better get the ice Nellie.

NELLIE: *AYAMARE!* (APOLOGIZE!)

YUMI: *Gomennasai? Gomennasai, GOMENnasai!*
    (I'm sorry? I'm sorry, I'm SORRY!)
    ごめんなさい？ごめんなさい、ごめんなさい！

EVELYN: GO, Nellie!

Nellie goes to get ice. Split stage. The kitchen is a tableau. Catherine is in the living room, sitting at her desk using the phone.

CATHERINE: Operator? Yes, Operator? Please put me through to Doctor Grant--

She rifles nervously through the drawers on her desk.

    Yes. I can hold, but it is somewhat urgent--
    Hello?
    Hello?

Catherine freezes. The kitchen comes back to life. Nellie rushes in with ice.

NELLIE: Here--

She hands the ice to Evelyn.

EVELYN: Thank you.

NELLIE: *AYAMARE.* (APOLOGIZE.)

YUMI: *Iya, antaga-yattanoni!*
    (No! You did this to me!)
    イヤ、アンタがやったのに！

NELLIE: What did she just say?

EVELYN: I don't speak Japanese--

YUMI: *Ayamaru-monka!*
    (I will not apologize!)
    謝るもんか！

51

NELLIE: Well, obviously--

YUMI: *Teo kegashitano! Kegashitano!*
     (My hand is broken! It's broken!)
     手を怪我したの！　怪我したの！

EVELYN: Oh, shhh, shhh, it's going to be okay, Yumi--
   (to Nellie) Can you pass me that dictionary?

Nellie gives Evelyn the dictionary. She looks through it as she holds the cold compress to Yumi's hand.

     Yoku naru? (Better?)

YUMI: *Te-ga--*
     (My hand--)
     手が・・・

She passes the dictionary back to Nellie.

EVELYN: Look up *te ga* (my hand.) It's easier if you do it--

NELLIE: I don't know if I can--

EVELYN: Look it up!

YUMI: *Nante hidoikoto-suruno? Dooshite?*
     (What have you done to me? What did you do?)
     何て酷いことするの？　どうして？

The kitchen freezes. The living room resumes activity. Catherine continues to look through the drawers.

CATHERINE: Yes, operator? The line is busy? Well, try again. This is an emergency.

She finally opens a small cubby in the desk and finds a paper crane. She looks at it intently.

     Yes. I'll hold, but--
     Operator?
     Operator?

She notices something on the inside of the crane. She begins to take it apart.

CATHERINE (Cont'd): What on earth? Is that writing?

She freezes. The kitchen scene resumes.

NELLIE: Oh, Evvie, when is the doctor going to get here?

EVELYN: I don't know, but we have to stay calm. Just keep smiling.

They look at Yumi and smile falsely. They say the next several lines through gritted teeth.

NELLIE: Should I get Alvin?

EVELYN: You don't want to bother him at work--

NELLIE: It is his wife.

EVELYN: The doctor bills alone will be the day's wages. You'd best not say anything. He's going to be upset as it is.

The kitchen freezes. Catherine opens all of the cranes and inspects them. The Ghosts gather around her. Catherine puts down the phone and frantically looks at the writing on the paper, though she cannot read it.

CATHERINE: Oh!

She picks up the phone.

> Yes, hello?
> You've got him?
> Yes, thank you--

She waits, still entranced by the secrets of the cranes. The Ghosts inch in closer and closer--

> Dr. Grant. There's been a bit of an accident.
> Yes, broken fingers. Maybe a broken hand? Can you come
by?
> Thank you, Doctor.

She hangs up. She inspects the writing with every one of her senses.

EVELYN (OFF): Mrs. Rhodes?

CATHERINE: One second--

She stares at them, trying to make sense of them. The Ghosts close in on her. She is suddenly very, very frightened.

EVELYN (OFF): Mrs. Rhodes?

CATHERINE: Coming!
     I'm coming Evelyn.

She tucks the cranes into her dress pocket. The lights go out suddenly.

SCENE EIGHT

Yumi and Catherine in the kitchen. The doctor has come and ban-daged her hand. Catherine is still rather nervous about being alone with Yumi.

CATHERINE: You're going to be alright.

Yumi is downtrodden.

Your hand is broken, but the doctor says you are alright--

Catherine looks in the dictionary. In Japanese she says:

Yoku natta? (Better now.)

Yumi nods. Alvin walks in through the kitchen door.

ALVIN: I'm home.

Yumi instinctively hides her hand.

CATHERINE: You're early.

ALVIN: Well hello to you, too.

CATHERINE: I'm sorry. Hello, Alvin.

ALVIN: How was your day?

CATHERINE: Fine.

ALVIN: Glad to hear it.

CATHERINE: Alvin I have something to tell you--

ALVIN: I take it playtime with the Prichetts was a success?

CATHERINE: In a manner of speaking--

ALVIN: Did Yumi learn to make a pie?

CATHERINE: Alvin--

55

ALVIN: I hope it's apple.
      Apple is my favorite.
      Where is it, hm?

CATHERINE: Alvin, I have to tell you. We had a bit of an--

ALVIN: Accident?
      Really?

CATHERINE: You know.

ALVIN: Dr. Grant called me at the lumberyard.

CATHERINE: I didn't want to bother you at work. It's her hand, it's-

He goes to Yumi.

      Let me see it.

CATHERINE: It looks as though Nellie--
      She broke her thumb and forefinger--

ALVIN: Let me see it.

Alvin pulls Yumi's arm up to inspect her hand.

CATHERINE: The doctor said it should heal up in a few weeks. She
    needs to rest it until then.

ALVIN: What happened?

CATHERINE: It was an accident.

ALVIN: What happened?

CATHERINE: Well you know the Prichetts. Nellie and Evelyn were
    bickering about one thing or another as they always do, and unfor-
    tunately, this time, Yumi's hand was in the path of a wayward
    rolling pin.
      I told you, Alvin. It was an accident.

Yumi looks visibly upset. Alvin says to her, in Japanese.

ALVIN: *Anata wa tsukarete iru. Moo yasumi nasai.* (You look tired. You should lie down.)

Yumi leaves.

CATHERINE: What did you just say to her?

ALVIN: She needs to rest.

Yumi exits.

What were you thinking bringing those girls here?

CATHERINE: I thought it would be good for her to meet some new people, I had no idea it would go awry. They are very sorry, believe me.

ALVIN: Do you think I'm simple?

CATHERINE: Nellie and Evelyn were teaching your wife how to bake you a pie. They were being friendly, honestly, which is more than I can say about anyone else around here.

ALVIN: Oh, really?

CATHERINE: Did you know about the looks I have been getting? The whispers in the marketplace. They are talking about you, about me. Our whole family.

ALVIN: You ought to be used to that.

CATHERINE: Not again.

ALVIN: After what happened with my father?

CATHERINE: I will not discuss this with you.

ALVIN: After you drove him out of our home? You should be plenty used to being the center of all the town gossip.

CATHERINE: Stop this, right now. You don't know what you are talking about.

ALVIN: And now you're been kicking up your heels with Dick every night? What a little tramp you've become--

CATHERINE: Pardon me, but I don't need to justify myself to you, or them, or anyone for that matter, and as for your father--

ALVIN: What about him?

CATHERINE: You are lucky I drove him out. You are lucky that you were too young to remember what it was like to have him under this roof--

ALVIN: Lucky to not remember what it was like to have a father? Yes. I bet I was the envy of every boy in Merced--

CATHERINE: Is that what you really want? To remember?

ALVIN: Yes--

CATHERINE: To remember him making you eat laundry soap until you vomited because you sassed him?

ALVIN: Enough.

CATHERINE: To remember him putting my head in the cupboard door and slamming it over and over because I burned the oatmeal?

ALVIN: Enough.

CATHERINE: To remember--

ALVIN: ENOUGH.

CATHERINE: It's a miracle we are even alive.

ALVIN: A miracle indeed.

CATHERINE: And I will not talk about this with you right now, or ever again. We are lucky he never came back that night. I hope he is dead.

No response.

CATHERINE (cont'd): As for the Prichetts, what those girls were doing, and I think you should be thankful for, is befriending your wife. If they like her, maybe everyone will start at least to accept her.

And this accident? That is all it was, Alvin.

When I invited the girls over, I honestly thought Yumi might make some friends. I hoped she might even learn some of the language--

ALVIN: From Nellie and Evelyn?

CATHERINE: Yes. Goodness. I'm willing to try anything, and if she learns from the Prichetts, it would certainly be easier than me sitting here with a blasted dictionary looking up every single word--

ALVIN: Dictionary?

CATHERINE: Yes. A dictionary.

She tosses the dictionary to Alvin nonchalantly.

ALVIN: Where did you get this?

CATHERINE: From Richard. Sheriff Regan gave it to him to give to me. He used to work at Manzanar?

ALVIN: I know who Sheriff Regan is. I'm just surprised he even gave you these. They're contraband.

CATHERINE: I know, but he thought that if I could talk to Yumi, she might have an easier time fitting in here.

ALVIN: I see. Well. I had no idea that you had such a desire to learn Japanese.

CATHERINE: Well, I never thought I'd ever have to--

ALVIN: --

CATHERINE: What?

ALVIN: Nothing.

CATHERINE: What's wrong?

ALVIN: Nothing--

CATHERINE: Was I not supposed to learn her language?

ALVIN: No, I--

CATHERINE: Is she not supposed to learn English like you prom-
ised she would?

ALVIN: I did, but--

CATHERINE: What am I to do with her, Alvin?

ALVIN: I don't know--

CATHERINE: Well?

ALVIN: I think--

CATHERINE: What?

ALVIN: I think it's good.

Catherine is surprised and relieved.

CATHERINE: Honestly?

ALVIN: Of course I do. I think it's very sweet of you.

CATHERINE: Good. I'm so glad to hear you say that.

ALVIN: But Japanese is a very hard language, you know.

CATHERINE: I know--

ALVIN: And it's going to take you a long time. Probably longer than
it took me.

CATHERINE: Perhaps.

ALVIN: So I'm going to hold on to this for you, that way, if you
have any questions, you can just ask me.

Alvin seems vaguely amused.

ALVIN (Cont'd): Try not to get too discouraged, alright?

CATHERINE: I will do my best.

ALVIN: Good night, Mother.

Alvin exits.

CATHERINE: Good night, Alvin.

Catherine looks to see that Alvin has left. She opens the dictionary and opens the small paper crane Yumi gave her. There is writing inside. The Ghosts enter.

> Discouraged?
> Hardly.

She takes out a piece of paper and a pen, and begins to translate. Lights up on Yumi in Catherine's office. She is writing, furiously. When she is done, she begins to fold the crane with her broken hand.

> "The island.
> Fight.
> Blood."

Yumi finishes the crane. The lights go down.

End of Act I.

Catherine paces anxiously in the kitchen. She looks through the door and walks away. She looks at the door, and walks away. She looks through the door, and sees Richard, coming up the walk.

CATHERINE: Hurry, Richard! We don't have much time.

RICHARD (OFF): I'm going as fast as I my feet can take me, Kitty. I'm just an old station master--

He comes in.

CATHERINE: Alvin gets home in an hour, and he cannot find out about this.

RICHARD: Find out about what?

CATHERINE: I have been hiding them for almost two months and--

RICHARD: Hiding what?

CATHERINE: Translating them in my spare time--

RICHARD: Translating what?

CATHERINE: But now, I am stumped. I cannot make any sense of it, no matter how hard I try, so I thought maybe you could take a look at them and see what you think--

RICHARD: Kitty! Slow down. What are you talking about?

CATHERINE: These.

She motions to the cranes.

RICHARD: Paper birds?

He picks up a crane and examines it.

CATHERINE: About thirty of them.

RICHARD: Did Yumi make all of them?

CATHERINE: As far as I know.

RICHARD: That's kind of incredible.

CATHERINE: Incredible is one word for it.
She means for me to read them. There is writing inside.

She opens a crane and shows it to him.

RICHARD: You read Japanese?

CATHERINE: Of course not.

RICHARD: Then how do you--

CATHERINE: With this.

RICHARD: Well, well, well. What do we have here? Looks like someone decided to take my advice after all.

CATHERINE: It was a matter of necessity. Now can we dispense with this chit chat? I need a second set of eyes--

RICHARD: So, I was right?

CATHERINE: Right about what?

Ignoring him, she goes and gets her notebook.

RICHARD: The dictionary.

CATHERINE: I do not have time for this.

RICHARD: Come on, admit it, I was right.

CATHERINE: Richard--

RICHARD: I won't help you 'til you tell me I was right.

CATHERINE: I do not need your help. I just need to pick your brain for a minute.

RICHARD: Well brain-picking and help cost the same price. And the price is admitting once and for all that I was right.

CATHERINE: You were right. Are you happy?

RICHARD: Was that so hard?

CATHERINE: Can we please concentrate on these cranes?

RICHARD: But I really was right--

CATHERINE: Richard!

RICHARD: Alright, alright.
　　　　　But first, can you at least tell me what I'm looking at?

Catherine opens the notebook and puts it on the table

CATHERINE: Like I said, the birds all have writing inside, so I have
　　　been scouring these dictionaries trying to figure out what they
　　　mean.
　　　　　These are my translations.

RICHARD: You did all this?

CATHERINE: Word by word. For months now.

RICHARD: You've been keeping this from me for months?

CATHERINE: Well, honestly, I didn't think anything of it, at first. It
　　　seemed like jumbled up thoughts, but now it seems like a puzzle I
　　　have only the corners of.

RICHARD: It seems like you're doing alright on your own. Why did
　　　you call me?

CATHERINE: In part to see if someone else can see what I'm miss-
　　　ing. But mainly because I couldn't keep this from you any longer.

RICHARD: Well, I'll admit, I would be a little miffed that you kept it
　　　from me at all if it wasn't so exciting.

CATHERINE: Exciting?

RICHARD: Come on Catherine, admit it. This is exciting. Translat-
　　　ing all these hidden letters. Reminds me of my days in the Great
　　　War.

CATHERINE: It does?

RICHARD: Ja. Ich spreche ein bisschen Deutsch. Sometimes they had me translate intercepted telegrams.

CATHERINE: When did you study German?

RICHARD: I didn't. I learned it from my grandfather. He came to the states right after the Civil War.

CATHERINE: Funny how we do that.

RICHARD: What?

CATHERINE: Mark our lives with the comings and goings of wars.

RICHARD: Never thought of it that way.

CATHERINE: Think about it. Translations remind you of the Great War. Your grandfather came here during the Civil War.
My son got married during this war.
I did not know that about you. That you speak German.

RICHARD: Well, that's because like your letters, I haven't told anyone else about it.

CATHERINE: Why is that?

RICHARD: It's not the most popular language nowadays. And I don't like reminding people that I'm German, even if it's just on the one side. Personally I wish my grandfather had been French. Then, I would be fluent in Francais. The language of amor.

CATHERINE: Oh really.

RICHARD: Yes, really. I'm a bachelor, you know.

CATHERINE: Oh yes. I am well aware.

A pause.

RICHARD: Boy. Look at all these. She's talented.

CATHERINE: Yes, and quite prolific. There seem to be more and more of them every day.

RICHARD: She just leaves them about?

CATHERINE: No. She puts them places. She hides them. I think she thinks its some kind of game.

RICHARD: What do you think it means?

CATHERINE: I was hoping you would help me find out.

RICHARD: You've had your nose to the grindstone for months. You probably don't need my help. Besides, I don't know anything about all these symbols. And I'm not as fast a study as I once was.

CATHERINE: If I can do it, you'll certainly be able to catch on fast enough.

RICHARD: You think so?

CATHERINE: Of course. It will be just you said. It'll be just like being back in the war translating those telegrams.
    You're right, you know.

RICHARD: Twice in one day? What about?

CATHERINE: This is exciting.

RICHARD: Alright. Let me see about making sense of these little characters here.

CATHERINE: Thank you.

She points to some of the writing.

    It's actually not so bad. Every picture looks a little like what its supposed to be. This one here, is an eye, and it looks a little like an eye--

RICHARD: You see an eye in this picture?

CATHERINE: I've been practicing.

RICHARD: I still can't believe you taught this to yourself.

CATHERINE: Well, it is not like I can ask Yumi for help, now look at this one, it's a tree—

He holds it up and examines it closely.

RICHARD: A tree, you say?

CATHERINE: Come on Richard. Use a little imagination. See? It's a tree.

RICHARD: Would you look at that? You're right--

A noise. Catherine leaps up.

CATHERINE: Did you hear that?

Catherine runs to the window. Footsteps coming up the walk.

Help me put these away.

Richard hands the cranes to Catherine who hides them.

RICHARD: What is going on?

Keys in the door.

CATHERINE: Alvin! He's home.

RICHARD: I know that. Is everything alright?

CATHERINE: It's just that, you know how he's been--

Alvin enters.

ALVIN: I'm home.

Alvin looks around.

Well, Hello, Dick.

RICHARD: Hello, Alvin.

ALVIN: What a pleasant surprise.

RICHARD: Good to see you too, son.

He extends his hand to shake and is rebuffed by Alvin.

      How are things at the lumberyard?

ALVIN: They're good. And at the train station?

RICHARD: Things are getting back to normal. It's nice to have so many of our young men finally come home.

ALVIN: Will you be joining us for dinner?

CATHERINE: Mr. Lindstrom is a busy man--

ALVIN: Nonsense. I bet he'd love to.

RICHARD: --

ALVIN: *(to Catherine)* What are you making?

CATHERINE: Oh. Nothing special. I think I'll just whip something together.

ALVIN: Swell. Then you'll stay?

RICHARD: Of course.

ALVIN: Let me go get Yumi. Have you met her yet?

RICHARD: Not yet. Your mother says she's rather shy.

ALVIN: She had an awful fright with those Prichett girls a few months back, and hasn't been too keen on meeting strangers without me.

RICHARD: I heard--

CATHERINE: It was an accident.

ALVIN: But I'm sure meeting some nice American folks will surely help put her at ease.

CATHERINE: The girls want to try and stop by again sometime soon and visit when her hand is better.

ALVIN: Well, we'll have to see how my wife feels about that.

RICHARD: How is her hand healing?

ALVIN: It is doing much better now. She's actually been practicing making these little paper birds to get her dexterity back--

CATHERINE: You don't say.

ALVIN: I'll have her bring one out for you. I bet she'd love for you to see it.
  (While exiting) Darling? I'm home!

He exits.

RICHARD: Well, he seems awfully chipper.

CATHERINE: Yes. He does.

RICHARD: Nice of him to invite me to stay.

CATHERINE: Yes. I hope you like beets.

RICHARD: Beets?

CATHERINE: It's what I've got to eat around here. That and a bologna sandwich.

RICHARD: I see you've been working on your victory garden--

CATHERINE: I have more important business to attend to.

Alvin reenters with Yumi. She is carrying a small paper crane.

ALVIN: And what business is that, mother?

CATHERINE: --

ALVIN: Well?

CATHERINE: I didn't want to spoil the surprise but--

ALVIN: Yes.

CATHERINE: I've been working on a wedding present for you.

She looks at Richard.

ALVIN: Really?

RICHARD: A wedding quilt.

ALVIN: I didn't know you quilted, mother.

Neither did she.

CATHERINE: Well, with all this time I've spent not having to go to work, I thought I would take up a new hobby.

ALVIN: Quilting.

CATHERINE: Yes. Quilting.
        Sewing a big wedding quilt.

RICHARD: It's a beaut.

CATHERINE: I am making it in all your favorite colors.

ALVIN: What colors are those?

CATHERINE: Red, of course. White, and green. Like your bedroom.

ALVIN: How thoughtful. Did you hear that Yumi? A quilt for us.

Yumi nods.

RICHARD: Did she bring the crane?

CATHERINE: Yes, I'd love to see it.

ALVIN: Well, since she was attacked, she's a bit worried that the ones she made aren't very good.

CATHERINE: Alvin, she was not attacked--

ALVIN: That's right. It was an accident.

RICHARD: Come on, you two.

ALVIN: Anyway, she's a little self-conscious--

RICHARD: I'm sure they're beautiful.

ALVIN: Oh, they are.
(To Yumi) Yumi, show it to Mr. Lindstrom.

Yumi nervously lifts her hands up to show the small origami bird.

YUMI: He-lo-ou.

RICHARD: Hello, Yumi. I'm Richard.

ALVIN: She's really come a long way.

CATHERINE: It's beautiful.

YUMI: *Arigatou.*
(Thank you.)
ありがとう。

CATHERINE: How did you make them?

ALVIN: *Doo yatte tsukutta?* (How did you make it?)

YUMI: *Kamio nandomo-nandomo otte...*
(I folded the paper over and over again--)
紙を何度も何度も折って・・・

ALVIN: She says she folded the paper--

YUMI: *Saigomade-ottara, tsuruno dekiagari.*
(And when I was finished, I had a crane.)
最後まで折ったら鶴の出来上がり。

ALVIN: And when she was finished, she had a crane.

71

YUMI: *An'mari umakunaikedo...*
   (It's not very good.)
   あんまり上手くないけど・・・

ALVIN: She says it isn't very good.

YUMI: *Demo renshuu-shiteru.*
   (But I've been practicing.)
   でも、練習してる。

ALVIN: But she's practicing.

YUMI: *Datte tsuruo-senba-ottara, watashino-negaiga kanaumono.*
   (And if I make a thousand cranes, my wish will come true.)
   だって鶴を千羽折ったら、私の願いが叶うもの。

ALVIN: It's her favorite thing to do.

CATHERINE: Can you ask her if she can teach Nellie and Evelyn?

ALVIN: *Ebrin to Nerii ni oshie te agetai desuka?* (Would you like to
   teach Evelyn and Nellie to make a crane?)
      You know, I don't think that it's such a good idea, Mother.
   She's still a little shaken up from the last time--

CATHERINE: Well, whenever she's ready.

YUMI: *Oshiete-agetaiwa.*
   (I actually think I would like to.)
   教えてあげたいわ。

RICHARD: What did she say?

ALVIN: That she's nervous about meeting them again.

YUMI: *Mada-takusan oranakya-naranaishi...*
   (I have so many to make still--)
   まだ沢山折らなきゃならないし・・・

ALVIN: But maybe someday, she'll want to.

CATHERINE: I don't think that's what she said.

YUMI: *Anohitotachini mooichido-aitaino.*
(I would like to see them again.)
あの人たちにもう一度会いたいの。

ALVIN: And how would you know?

RICHARD: It's her body language. You can tell a lot from the way a person moves. I learned that in the army. I didn't know what anyone was saying half the time. You just learn to read people.

ALVIN: Interesting. Interesting. I had no idea you were such an intuitive fellow.

RICHARD: Call it gut instinct, I guess.

ALVIN: Speaking of gut. I'm awfully hungry, Mother.

CATHERINE: Of course. Is bologna alright?

ALVIN: Sure. *(To Richard)* Sometimes I really miss the food overseas.

RICHARD: Oh really?

ALVIN: Most certainly. I think Uncle Sam makes a mighty fine sandwich.

RICHARD: You think so, huh?

ALVIN: Better than Mother's bologna.

RICHARD: Well at least when you're eating here, you aren't being shot at.

ALVIN: Although, Dick, admittedly I still do fear for my life.

RICHARD: I don't think I get your meaning.

ALVIN: What? You've had my mother's cooking.

RICHARD: And I am appreciative of it.

ALVIN: Who's not appreciative? All I'm saying is Mother, you could have worked a little harder in Home Ec--

Richard stands up from the table.

RICHARD: If you'll excuse me, Catherine, I have lost my appetite.

CATHERINE: I understand--

ALVIN: Come on, Dick. I'm just kidding around.

RICHARD: Good night, Catherine, Yumi. Alvin.

ALVIN: I'm just joking--

RICHARD: I do not find your brand of comedy particularly funny, Alvin.

ALVIN: Come on you ol' spoil sport. Kitty here can take a joke--

RICHARD: And I would thank you not to speak to your mother that way, even in jest. She has fed you, put a roof over your head--

CATHERINE: Richard, it's fine.

RICHARD: --She has taken care of you and of your wife when everyone else in the world would have turned you both out.

ALVIN: Actually, Dick, I pay the bills around here, I buy the food, pay the electric. So who is taking care of whom, exactly?

RICHARD: I have heard just about enough mouth from you, son.

ALVIN: So you're my father now?

CATHERINE: There will be no more fighting in my home. Stop it, both of you, now.

ALVIN: You hear, that Dick? My mother wants you to pipe down. Isn't that right?

CATHERINE: *(To Richard)* I don't need you to fight my battles for me.

RICHARD: Well, if you're going to let him speak to you that way in your home, I think you do.

CATHERINE: Richard--

ALVIN: What are you going to do about it?

RICHARD: I have half a mind to escort you from your mother's home this instant--

Alvin laughs hysterically.

ALVIN: Just try it. Try it! I have killed bigger men than you with my bare hands. Do you think I'm going to let you escort me from this home? Do you? DO YOU?

A pause, and then, surprisingly, he laughs.

> Why the faces, everyone? I'm just fooling around.

RICHARD: Catherine, Yumi, we need to leave--

CATHERINE: Richard?

ALVIN: You can go, but they're not going anywhere. I haven't eaten yet. I haven't been served my damn bologna sandwich.

RICHARD: Alvin Rhodes, I swear if I--

Richard approaches Alvin as though to fight.

CATHERINE: *(Furiously)* Richard, STOP. Can't you see he's doing this to goad us. He's been like this for weeks.
> Go home. I can handle my ungrateful son on my own.

ALVIN: Ungrateful? Women can't take a joke, can they, Dick?

RICHARD: Don't talk to me, don't you even look at me, you little--

CATHERINE: Goodnight, Richard.

RICHARD: But, Catherine--

CATHERINE: Goodnight, Richard.

Richard exits. Yumi is terrified.

ALVIN: What's eating him?

He looks for a response.

CATHERINE: Do you not see what kind of a monster you're becoming?

ALVIN: Mother--

CATHERINE: To drive him away like that? With those threats? With that horrible story?

ALVIN: What threat? I was kidding.

She goes to leave.

Now wait a second, mother--

CATHERINE: What now? What is it?

ALVIN: I apologize.
For what I said. About the food.

CATHERINE: I don't even know what to say to that. I don't. You disgust me.

Catherine exits.

SCENE TWO

Catherine alone, translating. Yumi is elsewhere on the stage, folding cranes. The Ghosts surround Catherine as she works.

YUMI: *Isoide.*
> (You must work faster.)
> 急いで。

CATHERINE: Fast.

YUMI: *Izure yatsuni-mitsukaru. Soonareba, hontooni-abunaino.*
> (He will find out about this eventually, and when he does, it will not be good for either of us.)
> いずれ奴に見つかる。そうなれば、本当に危ないの。

CATHERINE: Soldier.

YUMI: *Kyasarin.*
> (Catherine.)
> キャサリン。

Catherine looks up, as though she heard something, then looks right back down.

> *KYASARIN.* (CATHERINE.)
> キャサリン。

Chills run down Catherine's spine.

CATHERINE: Medic.

YUMI: *Watashiwa torawarenomi. Kokowa watashitachino roogoku.*
> (I am a hostage here. Held against my will in your home, now a prison for us both.)
> 私は囚われの身。ここは私たちの牢獄。

CATHERINE: Prisoner.

YUMI: *KYASARIN.*
> (CATHERINE.)
> キャサリン。

CATHERINE: Who's there?

YUMI: *Moshi-mitsukattara, yatsuni korosareru.*
      (If he finds out, he will kill us both.)
      もし見つかったら、奴に殺される。

CATHERINE: Who's there! I hear you. Come out.

Yumi comes out of her hiding place with another crane and a small box.

      Yumi.

Catherine is relieved.

      You frightened me. *Bikkuri shita.* (Frightened.) Don't sneak up on my like that.

YUMI: *Kore. Mite.*
      (Here. Take it.)
      これ。見て。

CATHERINE: What is this?

Catherine takes the crane, and sets it down. She opens the box. Inside is a thousand-stitch belt.

      Oh! You washed the belt. Thank you. I will find somewhere special for it--

She starts to put it back in the box.

YUMI: *Dame!*
      (No!)
      だめ！

CATHERINE: What?

YUMI: NO!

CATHERINE: What's wrong?

Yumi takes it back out. It is an obviously different belt.

CATHERINE (Cont'd): You made another one? I don't understand--

YUMI: *Hokanimo-aruno. Mitsuketano. Onegai...*
      (There are more. I found them. Please--)
      他にもあるの、見つけたの。お願い・・・

CATHERINE: What? What are you saying?

Yumi hands Catherine the crane.

YUMI: *Onegai, yonde.*
      (Please, read it.)
      お願い、読んで。

CATHERINE: Alright, I--

YUMI: *Onegai-shimasu.*
      (Please.)
      お願いします。

CATHERINE: I will. As soon as I can. *Hai* (Yes.)

Yumi disappears into the night. Catherine is left alone to translate. Suddenly, Richard's gentle knock at the door. Catherine puts away the cranes, and goes to the kitchen to let him inside.

RICHARD: Kitty, I couldn't sleep a wink. I had to know you were alright.

He embraces her.

CATHERINE: I'm fine. I have been handling Alvin's temper tantrums since he was two.

RICHARD: I know, but that was frightening. He's dangerous. This isn't a joke.

CATHERINE: I don't know what to make of it. Since he has been back he runs as hot and cold as a faulty faucet.

RICHARD: What are you still doing up?

CATHERINE: Working on the cranes.

RICHARD: Have you had any luck?

CATHERINE: Still working at a snail's pace, unfortunately.

RICHARD: You know, Sheriff Regan can probably--

CATHERINE: No. Absolutely not. I'm not bringing these to Howard. He'd probably haul us all away.

RICHARD: It's just a suggestion, Kitty.

CATHERINE: I will take it under advisement.
    Can I get you some coffee? I was planning on making a pot for myself. I am trying to finish as much of this crane as I can tonight. It reminds me a bit of examinations at Mills.

RICHARD: My college girl. How could I forget?

CATHERINE: And a lot of good it has done me.

RICHARD: I'm afraid I shouldn't have anything that will keep me up. I have an early day tomorrow.
    I really just wanted to see that you were alright.

CATHERINE: I'm fine. Really. I am.

RICHARD: I'll be keeping an eye on Alvin.

CATHERINE: I would appreciate that.

RICHARD: Kitty, I--
    Happy translating to you.

CATHERINE: Thank you. Have a good night.

RICHARD: Good night.

Richard exits.

SCENE THREE

In the kitchen, Lucille, Nellie, Evelyn and Catherine are talking. Something is clearly wrong with Evelyn.

LUCILLE: I am just so sorry about what happened last time--

NELLIE: No one is sorrier than me, believe me, Mrs. Rhodes. I felt just awful about all of it.

CATHERINE: It's alright.

LUCILLE: I do hope Yumi can forgive the girls.

CATHERINE: I think she already has. In fact, it was her idea to have the girls over to show them how to make these little paper cranes.

LUCILLE: Well, isn't that lovely?

CATHERINE: It's a hobby of hers.

LUCILLE: How thrilling.

NELLIE: I'm looking forward to it, aren't you, Evvie?

EVELYN: Hmm?
Oh, yes.

CATHERINE: Evelyn, is everything alright?

EVELYN: Of course, Mrs. Rhodes. Just a little tired is all.

LUCILLE: She still hasn't heard from Danny--

EVELYN: Mother!

LUCILLE: Well, you haven't. Not yet. She's a bit on edge.

EVELYN: I don't want to talk about it.

NELLIE: It's going to be alright.

EVELYN: We don't know that.

81

LUCILLE: No. We don't. But we go on. We go on living, for whatever that's worth, and today, you're living by making small paper
birds with Alvin's Jap--anese wife.

CATHERINE: I will run and get her.

*Catherine exits. Lights go up in the living room where Yumi is sit-
ting. She is surrounded by cranes.*

> Yumi?
> Yumi?
> The Prichetts are here. They've come to help you with the
> *tsuru* (cranes).

The lights come up in the kitchen.

EVELYN: Did you have to tell her that? About Danny?

LUCILLE: What? It's not a secret.

NELLIE: It is a little sensitive though, don't you think?

EVELYN: Really, Mother.

LUCILLE: Well forgive me for informing people of the reason for
your absentminded behavior.

EVELYN: Absentminded? Absentminded?

LUCILLE: Yes. Absentminded--

Catherine reenters with Yumi.

NELLIE: Hello, Yumi!

Nellie goes to Yumi and hugs her. Yumi is visibly uncomfortable.

> *Gomen nasai anata no te.* (I am sorry about your fingers.)

YUMI: Thank you.

EVELYN: Did you hear that?

82

LUCILLE: She said "Thank you!" She's catching on awfully quickly.

CATHERINE: We are very proud of her.

LUCILLE: Well, I'm off to the market.

CATHERINE: Alright. I'll send the girls home when they're finished here.

LUCILLE: Thanks again, for letting them come back after the last time.

CATHERINE: I'm sure it will all be fine.

LUCILLE: Goodbye!

CATHERINE AND THE PRICHETTS: Goodbye.

The girls and Yumi sit down at the kitchen table. Yumi hands them each a piece of paper.

CATHERINE: Now, girls, I need to step into the other room for a bit. I'm working on a letter. Do you mind?

NELLIE: No.

EVELYN: Not at all. We'll take good care of her.

CATHERINE: I will just be in the other room if you need me.

NELLIE: Alright.

Catherine exits. The girls watch Yumi intently as she shows them how to delicately fold a paper crane.

In the next room, Catherine takes out the dictionary and letters. The Ghosts enter.

Back in the kitchen, Evelyn looks onto Nellie's work.

EVELYN: You're doing it wrong.

NELLIE: No I'm not.

EVELYN: You fold this one first.

She shows it to Yumi.

This one first, right, Yumi?

Yumi nods.

See? Fold in, and then back out.

In the living room the Ghosts resume where they had left off. One man dead, one man in charge and the rest in peril. Catherine slowly clunks through the translation, word by word.

CATHERINE: Eye.
Sound.
Fight.

An interpretation of these words in movement.

In the kitchen, the girls fold. There is a small stack of cranes next to Yumi.

EVELYN: She's so fast!

NELLIE: I know. Look at mine.

A sad little crane.

It doesn't have a head.

YUMI: *Moo-ichido.*
(Try again.)
もう一度。

She motions for her to try again, handing her a slip of paper.

EVELYN: Yours is terrible, but look at mine. The wings are lop-sided.

She shows the crane to Yumi. Yumi makes a minor adjustment and hands it back to her.

Thank you.

YUMI: *Tsuzukete.*
    (Keep going.)
    続けて。

In the office, Catherine is making little headway on the translation.

CATHERINE: Knife.
    Cries.
    Kills.

The Ghosts mime the words.

The girls in the kitchen keep folding. Each girl now has a small pile of cranes in front of them.

EVELYN: Yumi?

Yumi looks up.

    How many?

YUMI: *Tsuzukete.*
    (Keep going.)
    続けて。

NELLIE: Gee whiz, my fingers are tired. How does she not get tired doing this?

EVELYN: I don't know.

NELLIE: I think I'm finished.

YUMI: *Tsuzukete.*
    (Keep going.)
    続けて。

NELLIE: What did she say?

EVELYN: I think she wants us to keep working.

NELLIE: I can't work anymore, I'm hungry.

EVELYN: Nellie. It's impolite.

NELLIE: Impolite or not, I need something to eat, and we know there's nothing here.

EVELYN: There might be something--

NELLIE: Please.

EVELYN: Well-

NELLIE: I am really hungry.

EVELYN: Then go talk to Mrs. Rhodes.

NELLIE: Can't you--

EVELYN: Nellie. I'm busy.

NELLIE: Of course you are.

She goes to leave.

EVELYN: Oh, and Nellie? While you're in there, can you see if she has the dictionary? I want to ask Yumi about the cranes.

NELLIE: Fine. FINE.
I just hope she has a hard candy for me to suck on.

Nellie enters the living room and startles Catherine.

Mrs. Rhodes?

CATHERINE: Goodness! Hello! Yes, Nellie?

NELLIE: I know this is kind of a long shot, but do you have anything here to eat?

CATHERINE: I think there are some sardines in the cupboard. I might also have some Ovaltine. I'll come in and fix it for you.

NELLIE: No, no. Don't get up. I can get it.

CATHERINE: Thank you.

Nellie turns around to go back, and then remembers.

NELLIE: Oh! Mrs. Rhodes?

CATHERINE: Yes?

NELLIE: Evelyn wanted to borrow the dictionary if you still have it. She wanted to ask Yumi about the cranes. We weren't sure how many of them she wanted us to make, and my hands are getting awfully tired--

CATHERINE: I don't have it with me.

NELLIE: No?

CATHERINE: No.

NELLIE: Well, where is it? Maybe I can look for it.

CATHERINE: I am not sure.

Catherine begins acting strangely. Nellie catches on.

NELLIE: Did you lose it?

CATHERINE: No.

NELLIE: Did you have to give it back to Mr. Lindstrom?

CATHERINE: No.

Nellie walks over to Catherine. Catherine begins covering up her translations with her arms and other papers.

NELLIE: It'd be a shame if you lost it.

Nellie sees the dictionary and the letters.

Mrs. Rhodes? What are you working on?

CATHERINE: A letter. To my friend, Sandy.

NELLIE: With a Japanese dictionary?

CATHERINE: Nellie, I--

NELLIE: I thought you said you didn't have it.

CATHERINE: I don't. Not the old one--
      Anyway, this is none of your business!

NELLIE: What are all those? Are they Yumi's? What are you doing?

CATHERINE: Nothing. I don't know. I'm still trying to figure it out myself.

NELLIE: Figure what out, Mrs. Rhodes?

CATHERINE: You can't tell anyone you saw this.

NELLIE: Is everything alright?

CATHERINE: It's fine.

NELLIE: Are you sure?

CATHERINE: Yes. Of course.

NELLIE: Because--

CATHERINE: You should leave.

Catherine tucks all the letters into the dictionary and shoves it into the desk.

NELLIE: Mrs. Rhodes, I--

CATHERINE: Now. You should leave now. I have to get to the market before Alvin gets home.

NELLIE: We can go for you, if you want--

CATHERINE: That's very kind, but no. You have to go.

NELLIE: Alright.

CATHERINE: And please, Nellie. Don't tell anyone about this.

NELLIE: Alright, alright, I won't--

CATHERINE: Do you promise?

NELLIE: Yes.

CATHERINE: Good. Get your sister and go home for lunch.

NELLIE: But--

CATHERINE: GO!

NELLIE: I'm going!

Nellie rushes into the kitchen.

We have to leave--

EVELYN: But--

NELLIE: Now.

EVELYN: Alright. Goodbye, Yumi--

Nellie practically drags Evelyn out.

YUMI: Good-bye.

NELLIE: Come on!

EVELYN: I'm coming. Sheesh!

NELLIE: You'll never guess what I just saw.

SCENE FOUR

It is night. Catherine is still working fastidiously on the translation. After a few moments, she suddenly has some clarity.

The lights come on suddenly.

ALVIN: Mother?

CATHERINE: Alvin, I--

She tries to nonchalantly put away the letters.

> What are you doing up?

ALVIN: I heard some rustling around and I thought I would see what it was.

CATHERINE: You really are the man of the house.

ALVIN: What are you working on?

CATHERINE: I'm writing a letter. To a friend of mine.

ALVIN: Oh?
Which friend?

CATHERINE: You remember Sandy.

ALVIN: Of course

CATHERINE: She's offered to send me a pattern. For the quilt.

ALVIN: That's wonderful.

CATHERINE: Yes.

ALVIN: So late at night?

CATHERINE: I suppose so.
I couldn't sleep.

ALVIN: You should make yourself some warm milk.

CATHERINE: That's a good idea. I'll go do that.

She gets up to go, but Alvin blocks her path.

Excuse me.

ALVIN: Not so fast.

CATHERINE: What's wrong?

ALVIN: Why are you really awake?

CATHERINE: I told you, I couldn't sleep. I had a letter to write--

ALVIN: What are you really working on?

He walks over to her desk and begins rifling through her things.

CATHERINE: Alvin, this is ridiculous.

ALVIN: I'm only curious.

CATHERINE: What I do at my desk on my time is none of your business--

ALVIN: I want you to be honest with me.

CATHERINE: I am being honest--

ALVIN: Where's the dictionary?

CATHERINE: The dictionary--

ALVIN: Where is it?

CATHERINE: I don't know.

ALVIN: I heard today that you were acting really strangely toward the Prichett girls.

CATHERINE: It's not what you think.

ALVIN: They said that I should check on you.

CATHERINE: They did, did they?

ALVIN: That I should ask you about the letters. About the dictionary. Why you've been acting so oddly.

CATHERINE: I don't know what they were talking about.

ALVIN: You're lying!

CATHERINE: Alvin--

ALVIN: You're lying to me.

CATHERINE: I am not lying to you. Now let me go this instant--

ALVIN: Where are they?

CATHERINE: Where are what?

ALVIN: The cranes.

CATHERINE: What cranes?

ALVIN: The ones Yumi's been making.

CATHERINE: Why? Why do you care?

ALVIN: I just want to see them.

CATHERINE: They are all over the place, Alvin. Just look around. They are everywhere.

Alvin finds a crane.

I do not see what all the intrigue is about. They are just little paper birds--

He opens it. Catherine's stomach drops.

ALVIN: With writing inside. How sweet.
How many are there?

CATHERINE: Not that many, but like I said, I--

ALVIN: Let me see them.

CATHERINE: I don't see what all the fuss is about--

ALVIN: Let me SEE them.

Catherine goes slowly to her desk. She takes out the letters, deliberately leaving the one Yumi gave her with the belt behind.

CATHERINE: Here.

She hands them to him with the dictionary.

ALVIN: What do you know?

CATHERINE: Nothing, I can't make sense of the letters, the sounds—

ALVIN: What do you know?

CATHERINE: I could get one, maybe two words in at best.

ALVIN: And what were they?

CATHERINE: What were what?

ALVIN: The words.

CATHERINE: This is ridiculous.

ALVIN: What were they?

CATHERINE: Something about an eye. Yours, I imagine.

Catherine halts.

    I was just trying to--

ALVIN: Quiet!

She is. Alvin reads.

    What else does it say?

CATHERINE: I really don't know, it's all piecemeal, I can't--

ALVIN: Who else knows about this?

CATHERINE: Just the Prichett girls.

ALVIN: No one else?

CATHERINE: No--

ALVIN: Good. Good.

Alvin begins to tear them.

CATHERINE: Alvin, what are you doing?

ALVIN: Something that should have been done a long time ago--

CATHERINE: Destroying them?

ALVIN: YES.

CATHERINE: But why?

ALVIN: That is not of your concern.

CATHERINE: Stop it, Alvin. This is ridiculous. There's nothing in those letters that--

ALVIN: Shut up.

CATHERINE: Alvin?

ALVIN: What?

CATHERINE: Alvin, what is in those letters that they have to be destroyed?

ALVIN: It's not your business.

CATHERINE: Fine. Then I'm calling Sheriff Regan. I bet he would be thrilled to tell me whose business it is--

She goes to the phone. Alvin intercepts her. He throws the phone against the wall.

ALVIN: You will do no such thing.

CATHERINE: I will do as I please. If you will not let me call him, I will walk down to the station and tell him in person.

ALVIN: You will not--

CATHERINE: You cannot stop me.

A pause.

ALVIN: You're right. I can't.

CATHERINE: Why can't you just tell me what you think those letters say?

ALVIN: Because--

CATHERINE: What? What is it? You can tell me.

ALVIN: They're evidence.

CATHERINE: Evidence of what?

ALVIN: I shouldn't even tell you this.

CATHERINE: Go on. It is alright.

ALVIN: Yumi. She was captured on Okinawa.

CATHERINE: Oh my stars.

ALVIN: She was a POW.

CATHERINE: Yumi?

ALVIN: When we were out on recon, me and my buddy, John Westin, we come upon this little MASH tent in the woods.

CATHERINE: Alvin, I--

ALVIN: So we go up to it, we are just going to take everything really quietly, bring 'em all back in to camp. They're medical. We figure they don't have any serious weapons--

CATHERINE: But--

ALVIN: As we're about to capture it, John steps on a stick, and suddenly all eyes are on us. Guns. So I put my hands up, calm and collected, but John starts to lose it. He fires and they attack! He kills two of the unarmed men.

CATHERINE: Oh my gracious, Alvin, that's terrible. Why didn't you tell me?

ALVIN: Because it only gets worse.

CATHERINE: Alvin--

ALVIN: I grab John from behind to stop him from shooting these people. He's pretty surprised, of course, so he drops his weapon and we go hand-to-hand right there in front of the tent, in front of the enemy. Next thing I know, I'm pinned to the ground. John's hands around my neck. His weight crushing my throat--
      So I pull my knife from my belt, and I push it into him. I stab him with it, and keep pushing until my hands are inside his body. I felt his guts wrapped around my fingers.
      The rest, after seeing what I had done to another American soldier, surrender, including this nurse with beautiful brown eyes--

CATHERINE: Yumi.

ALVIN: Yumi.

He pauses.

      I hold the hostages at the tent for a few hours while I wait for backup, but after a while, it started to get dark, so I decide to walk them back to base. And as we're going along one of them must have broken off part of a stick. He held it in his hand, pretending to be injured, and when I went to see what was wrong he gouged me in the eye, and in a panic, I shot him. I had to.

CATHERINE: I know. Of course you did--

ALVIN: Thankfully, I had Yumi there. She took pity on me, tended to my eye. The other guy I was guarding ran off. She got me back to camp.

Catherine softens.

So you see, Mother? Why I couldn't tell you all this?

CATHERINE: I do.

ALVIN: I was so ashamed of killing those people. Of killing John--

CATHERINE: Is that what you think is in the letters?

ALVIN: I'm sure of it. I'm sorry I had to tell you like this. I never wanted you to know what kind of a monster I was over there.

CATHERINE: I know, sweetheart, I know.

ALVIN: And I know that it hasn't been easy. Having me back, I mean.

CATHERINE: No, it hasn't. But it's alright. I'm so sorry. I had no idea.

ALVIN: How could you?
       Can we go to bed now, Mother? I'm very tired.

CATHERINE: Of course we can, darling.

Alvin goes to leave.

ALVIN: Aren't you going to bed?

CATHERINE: In just a moment. I think I need that warm milk after all.

Alvin kisses her on the cheek.

ALVIN: Good night.

CATHERINE: Good night, darling.

Alvin exits. When Catherine is sure he has gone to bed, she goes back to her desk and takes out the page of the letter she was working on. She deliberates, and then throws it away. The Ghosts reappear, reassembling the crane. They leave it for her to find.

SCENE FIVE

Lights up on a happy Alvin and Catherine, and Yumi at the kitchen table.

ALVIN: --And then, Robert Jones, you remember him right, mother?

CATHERINE: You went to high school together, right?

ALVIN: Right. Well he's my manager now that he's back from overseas.

CATHERINE: Go on--

ALVIN: But he spends most of his time goofing off like a teenager. So he was clowning around again down by the log saw and he drops his lunch box right into it. The thing wound up getting jammed right in there. We lost three hours of work trying to fix it. I was furious so I went to Tom, and I told him that I was at least as valuable as Robert Jones, and probably more cost effective, and he agreed! He gave me a raise on the spot. And Robert's job. I got a promotion. Can you believe it?

CATHERINE: Well. That's really something.

ALVIN: What? You're not happy?

CATHERINE: Of course I'm happy. Of course I am.
       I'm just glad to see you smile.

ALVIN: What's not to smile about? Things are swell.

CATHERINE: That's true.

ALVIN: And I have even better news.

CATHERINE: Oh yeah?

ALVIN: Yumi and I--

He puts his arm around her. Catherine winces.

       Are moving!

He kisses her on the cheek.

CATHERINE: That's wonderful, Alvin.

ALVIN: Now that I have that promotion, we can finally afford it.

CATHERINE: I'm so happy for you.

ALVIN: Thanks, Mother. All that's left now is the pitter patter of little feet.

CATHERINE: She isn't.
Is she?

ALVIN: Not yet, but maybe by spring. Who knows?

CATHERINE: That would be wonderful. I'm so excited for you. Omedetou, Yumi.

YUMI: Thank you.

ALVIN: You know, I forgot to check the mail on my way in. I'll be back in a moment.

CATHERINE: Oh, alright.

Alvin exits.

Coffee, Yumi? Tea?

Yumi shakes her head no.

I'm going to fix myself some tea.

She stands up. Yumi grabs her by the dress.

Hmm?

Yumi hands Catherine another paper crane.

Oh.
What is it?

Yumi motions for her to open it. Catherine unfolds the crane. There is writing inside. The Ghosts appear.

CATHERINE (Cont'd): Yumi?
Yumi, what is this?
Yumi hands her the dictionary.
You want me to translate this?
Why?

Yumi hands her a small bundle.

YUMI: *Anatawa hontoono-kotoo-shiranaino.*
(The truth you know is not truth.)
あなたは、本当の事を知らないの。

CATHERINE: What?

YUMI: *Yatsuno-hanashiwa, minna-uso.*
(What your son has told you is a lie.)
奴の話は、みんな嘘。

CATHERINE: I don't understand--

Yumi exits. Catherine stuffs the letter in her pocket. Alvin reenters.

ALVIN: Where's Yumi?

CATHERINE: She went to your room, I think.

ALVIN: Is everything alright?

CATHERINE: Of course, Alvin. Why wouldn't it be?

ALVIN: When is dinner?

CATHERINE: In about an hour?

ALVIN: I'll go talk with her.

CATHERINE: Is ham okay? It'll be nice to celebrate.

ALVIN: Sure. Ham is great.

CATHERINE: Alright.

Alvin exits. Catherine looks at the crane. She takes it into her office. She begins to translate. Yumi appears.

YUMI: *Yatsuwa nakamao-mite, "Anoko"tte watashio yubi-sashita. Watashiwa wakega-wakaranakatta. Totemo kowakatta.*
> (He looked at his friend. He pointed at me, as if to say, "I'll take that one." I didn't understand him. I was so scared.)
> 奴は仲間を見て、『あの子』って私を指差した。私は訳が分からなかった。とても怖かった。

CATHERINE: Scared?

YUMI: *Soshite yatsuwa jyuuo nakamani-muketa. "Yamero!"tte sakenderunoni. Demo, nihatsu-utta. Ippatsuwa fuzake-nagara.*
> (So he raised his gun. He raised it against his own cohort who once again was crying "No!" He shot him twice. Once for spite.)
> そして奴は銃を仲間に向けた。『やめろ！』って叫んでるのに。でも二発撃った。一発はふざけながら。

CATHERINE: Gun.
> No?
> The bundle--

Inside is a set of American dog tags.

> John Westin? Why would--

She sees that the tags are wrapped in yet another Thousand-Stitch Belt.

> A third belt?
> Oh my God. No.
> Alvin. No!

Catherine picks up the phone.

> Operator? Yes, hello. Would you put me through to Sheriff Regan please?
> Thank you.

She waits.

CATHERINE (Cont'D):   Sheriff Regan? Hello, it's Catherine Rho-
    des.
    No, no, everything is fine. I just--
    It's just--
    It's--
    Nothing.
    Nothing at all. I'm sorry to have bothered you.

SCENE SIX

Catherine and Richard are at the kitchen table.

CATHERINE: I have told myself over and over again that this is the right thing to do--

RICHARD: And it is.

CATHERINE: Then why does it feel so awful? So wrong?

RICHARD: Because he's your son.

CATHERINE: He is.

A pause.

RICHARD: You know, Catherine--

CATHERINE: Stop.

RICHARD: You don't even know what I was going to say.

CATHERINE: I know you well enough to know that you were about to say something sweet. Something touching. Something about always being there for me.

RICHARD: Well--

CATHERINE: I don't need you to say anything. I am just glad you are here.

RICHARD: You don't know that I was going to say anything about being there for you. You don't know that I was going to be sweet--

CATHERINE: I do.

RICHARD: Oh, really?

CATHERINE: Because I know you like the back of my hand.

RICHARD: Well, I hate to tell you this, but this one time, you would be wrong.

CATHERINE: Would I?

RICHARD: Because I was actually going to tell you that you had spinach in your teeth.

CATHERINE: Spinach? I don't eat spinach.

RICHARD: The spinach from your victory garden--

CATHERINE: I don't have a victory garden--

RICHARD: And that even with it wedged between those two pearly whites--

CATHERINE: Enough--

RICHARD: You're beautiful.

He kisses her.

   Now, let me make sure I got all the spinach out.

CATHERINE: There was never any spinach.

RICHARD: And yet, you let me kiss you. How strange.

CATHERINE: Apparently, I've lost my mind.

A pause.

RICHARD: You're making the right decision, Catherine.

CATHERINE: You think so?

RICHARD: I do--

A knock at the kitchen door.

CATHERINE: What on earth?

RICHARD: Who is it?

CATHERINE: I don't know.

EVELYN (OFF): Mrs. Rhodes! Mrs. Rhodes? Are you home?

CATHERINE: One second.

Catherine opens the door. Evelyn bursts in carrying a large paper bag.

      Evelyn? Is everything alright?

EVELYN: Everything is more than alright--

Evelyn sees Richard.

      Oh, hello, Mr. Lindstrom!

RICHARD: Hello, Evelyn.

EVELYN: I have the most wonderful news.

CATHERINE: What is it?

EVELYN: Well, remember that day Nellie and I were making birds with Yumi?

CATHERINE: Of course--

EVELYN: Well, I wanted to ask her why she was making all of them—

CATHERINE: And?

EVELYN: Well, I never got the chance to actually ask her, so I went and asked Sheriff Regan about them the next day, and I found out that the Japanese believe that if you make a thousand of these paper cranes, a wish you have will come true.

RICHARD: That's fascinating--

EVELYN: Anyway, I had already made about six of them, so I thought I would make the whole lot.

CATHERINE: You made a thousand paper birds? All by yourself?

106

EVELYN: Cranes, actually, and yes, I did. I stayed up every night for two weeks, and finally, I finished. See!

She takes out the cranes and shows them to Richard and Catherine.

CATHERINE: Oh my goodness. Look at those cranes.

EVELYN: I came to show Yumi!

CATHERINE: She's at the doctor's with Alvin right now, but if you want to come by later--

EVELYN: Of course! I have to thank her.

RICHARD: Whatever for?

EVELYN: Because--

She takes an envelope out of her bag.

Look!

Richard takes the envelope and shows it to Catherine.

RICHARD: It's from Danny.

CATHERINE: Oh my stars. Danny?

EVELYN: He's coming home! He was captured in a battle, and put in a POW camp for months, but then he was rescued! He's been in the hospital for a while, and then on a ship, so he never got to send me a letter, but he's going to be fine. He's already here in the states. He's coming home this week. Can you believe it?

CATHERINE: This is wonderful news!

EVELYN: We are to be married in June. This June. He said so in the letter.

RICHARD: Congratulations.

EVELYN: And it's all thanks to Yumi and her cranes.

CATHERINE: I knew he'd come home to you, Evvie.

EVELYN: I'm so glad you were right.
       Well, I suppose I'll drop by later and show Yumi all my hard
  work.

CATHERINE: See you then.

EVELYN: Goodbye, Mrs. Rhodes. Mr. Lindstrom.

RICHARD: Goodbye, Evelyn.

CATHERINE: Good bye!

She exits.

RICHARD: That is the most wonderful news.

CATHERINE: Indeed.

A pause. Richard hands the phone to Catherine.

RICHARD: It's time.

CATHERINE: I know.

RICHARD: I'm here if you need me.

CATHERINE: Thank you.

She dials.

       Operator?
       Please patch me through to Sheriff Regan. It's urgent.

A final explosion of cherry blossoms as The Ghosts take the stage, they tell the story of Yumi and Alvin as Yumi reads her letter in Japanese. Catherine reads right behind her in English.

CATHERINE: His ally stood apart from him, shaking his head no, no! I knew the word, for he exclaimed it with intensity.

That was when he raised his weapons against my unarmed colleagues. One by one, he shot all except another nurse who quivered in fear. He tied her to a tree.

YUMI: *Sonoatowa, moo-omoidashitakumo-nai. Yatsuwa watashio-tsukande beddoni-taoshi, karadao oshitsukete-kita. Subeteno-bubun-o kanjirareru-yooni. Sokowa, nijikan-maeni, chimamireno-heishiga-shinda beddo-datta. Namagusai-chiga, fukuni- shimik-onde-kita.*

(What happened next was brutal. He grabbed me and pressed himself to me, making sure I could feel every part of him he wanted me to feel. He lay me down on one of the hospital cots, where not two hours before, a man had bled to death in my care. His wet, sticky blood seeped through my clothing.)

その後はもう思い出したくもない。奴は私を掴んでベッドに倒し、体を押し付けてきた。すべての部分を感じられるように。そこは二時間前に、血まみれの兵士が死んだベッドだった。生臭い血が、服に染み込んできた。

CATHERINE: He ravaged me there, at gunpoint, with the other nurse watching. When she screamed for help, he shot her. I felt that she had been the lucky one of us two.

YUMI: *Yatsuga kio-sorashiteiru-sukini, watashiwa-mesuotori, yat-suga-kochirao- muita-toki, hidari-meni-tsukisashite nigeyooto-shita. Demo yatsuwa-tsuyoku, ikari-kurutteite, moo nanimo-dekinakatta.*

(While he was distracted, I grabbed a scalpel from the medical tray next to me. When he turned back, I gouged his eye, blinding him. I began to run, but he was strong, and furious.)

奴が気をそらしている隙に私はメスを取り、奴がこちらを向いた時、左目に突き刺して逃げようとした。でも奴は強く、怒り狂っていてもう何も出来なかった。

CATHERINE: He led me at gunpoint back to a camp full of men. He told them nothing of what I'd done, which surprised me. I was certain I was going to face death at the hands of this savage man, but instead, he took me for his bride.

YUMI: *Watashiwa koogi-surukotomo, tatakaukotomo-dekinakatta. Kotoba-mo tsuujinakatta. Demo, itsuka yatsuni fukushuu-suruto chikatta. Watashino-meiyono-tame, tomono-tame, soshite nihonno -tameni.*
> (I could not protest, I could not fight. There were no words they would understand. No words I understood. But I vowed that someday, I would have his life. For taking my honor, my colleagues, my homeland all from me.)
> 私は抗議することも、闘うこともできなかった。言葉
> も通じなかった。でもいつか奴に復讐すると誓った。
> 私の名誉のため、友のため、そして日本のために。

CATHERINE: *(Stops abruptly.)*
> That is where it ends?
> Alvin, what have you done--
> What have you done?

Catherine collapses under the weight of enormous sadness. She weeps.

Alvin is led away in handcuffs as Yumi looks on.

Yumi stands taking out a knife. She cuts into her own stomach as the lights go down.

End of play.

www.ingramcontent.com/pod-product-compliance
Lightning Source LLC
LaVergne TN
LVHW021402080426
835508LV00020B/2413